ASHER, MY SON

A YEAR IN THE LIFE OF A CHILDLESS FATHER

KAVIN J. LEY

FOREWORD

My first encounter with pregnancy loss came unexpectedly, as it usually does. My best friend was pregnant, and we were all eagerly waiting to meet her sweet son. And then he was gone. They had to say goodbye before they even said hello. I didn't know what to say or do or how to react. No parents should have to bury their baby.

A little time passed, and another friend lost her pregnancy. And another friend. And another friend. It was so life changing for them and their families. I tried my best to support them through their grief, and I held my daughter a little bit closer. I was so thankful that she was happy and healthy. When our oldest was just nine months old, we unexpectedly found ourselves pregnant with baby number two. After the initial shock wore off, we settled into the idea of two girls, just eighteen months apart and dug our heels in for the ride we were about to start.

And then, one morning, I woke up and Norah did not.

I tried all the things they instruct pregnant moms to do when a baby isn't moving as much: drink ice water, lay on your left side, drink juice, wait… I also tried to yell at her and use her name; to shake my belly and wake her up. I tried so hard not to panic, but deep in my heart, I knew something was wrong. I called my OB, my husband, and my mom. Within a few minutes, it was decided that I needed to head to the hospital to check on Norah. I packed up big sis and brought her with me to the hospital so that we could see what was going on. When the girl at the front desk wrote "decreased fetal movement" on a slip of paper to give to the nurse, I wanted to yell at her and tell her she was wrong. NO movement is not the same as decreased movement, but no one wants to hear you say that you are afraid your baby has died.

I was settled into a triage room and reassured the nurses that there was still no movement from Norah. Those nurses tried so hard to find her heartbeat. At 38 ½ weeks, it should have been easy. Soon, my husband arrived, followed by my mom, and eventually my physician. An ultrasonographer joined us in the room. When we finally saw Norah's sweet little body, it became glaringly evident her heart was still. My physician told us so gently that her heart had stopped and that she had died.

Our world stopped.

I only remember pieces of the next few hours and days. I remember making phone calls.

"I don't know how to say this."

"Norah has died."

"I'm starting my maternity leave, but it's not what we expected."

"We don't know what happened."

"I can't believe this is happening."

I remember my grandmother bringing a huge pot of chicken noodle soup. Neighbors I had not yet met brought us a basket of fruit. There were so many cards in the mail, phone calls, texts, private messages on social media, and condolences from friends near and far. There were also phone calls to and from those friends who truly understood the path down which we were just starting to journey.

Before we left the hospital, I asked for the name and phone number of a photographer.

Someone drove us and our vehicles home. We immediately put away the bassinet and the breast pump from our bedroom. I couldn't change anything else yet. I sat in Norah's nursery and cried. I grieved that I would never get to lay her in her crib or listen to her soft breath while she slept.

That evening, we were joined in our home by family and friends as we began to plan our goodbye. The photographer came and took pictures of us and my belly—my belly that had been so full of life 24 hours earlier.

The next morning, we returned to the hospital. We were greeted by one of the kindest and strongest nurses that I would meet along this journey. She walked us through the induction process with patience and grace. She held my hand and cried with me. She kept me comfortable and answered my questions. Norah was not born on her shift, so we were then able to meet our night nurse, who was thoughtful and compassionate. After our sweet, silent six-pound fifteen-ounce Norah was born, she guided us through her bath and helped direct our flow of visitors in and out of the room. My second nurse allowed us time to grieve our beautiful girl. She gave us space to follow the instructions of our friends, to *do* things with her.

Her daddy and I both read to her. I sang to her. He danced with her since he wouldn't get to dance with her at her wedding someday. Norah met so many of our loved ones. She met her grandparents, her big sister, her aunts and uncles, her extended family and many friends. We had eighteen hours to make a lifetime of memories with her.

In the six years since Norah died, I have changed so much. Norah was followed by a joyful little sister just over a year later. I have learned that hard things are worth doing, even when they are scary.

Norah's name means "honor" and "light." Each time I share her story or provide support to a hurting family, I believe I am able to honor her and give her life more weight.

Through my job as a patient care technician, I met Asher and his lovely parents. With a newfound passion for bereavement care, I have been blessed to meet many parents at the beginning of their journey through grief. I consider it to be the greatest honor to be able to walk alongside parents like Kavin and Betsy. Hopefully, I can carry a little bit of their burden, even if it is only for a brief time.

—Cori McKenzie

ACKNOWLEDGMENTS

I want to offer my sincerest words of thanks to Mom and Dad, Ashton and Ryne, Brittney, Andy and Kathy, Emily and James, Abby and Rodrigo, our extended family, and our friends for their love and support through our journey of loss. We could not have made it without you.

I want to give special thanks to Cori for being an important part of Asher's story and for contributing the foreword to this book.

I want to thank Beth Martin for formatting this book. I cannot fully express my appreciation for your expertise and generosity.

And I want to thank Betsy. You are my everything. Through all the ups and downs, we grow closer together. I cannot imagine going through this life with anyone else. There will never be enough words to tell you how much you mean to me. Asher and I love you more than you know. Thank you for being the greatest part of my life.

I also would like to extend my humblest of thanks to those who have generously provided resources, which have allowed for the publication of this book:

Brent & Karna Ley
Andy & Kathy Hart
Ashton & Ryne Hicks
Jes & Ian McConville
Larry & Jean Sheets
Matt & Allison Leonhardt
Neil & Wendy Laymon
Kaity Garrett
Sarah & James Rude in loving memory of
Gwendolyn Rose Rude
Trinity Episcopal Church, Fort Wayne, IN

and all the other generous individuals who gave money to help share Asher's story.

April 14, 2016

As soon as I got the call, I knew that I needed to write. For a few months, I debated starting a journal that could be shared with future family members, friends, or anyone who may be interested in listening to the ramblings of a "normal American man." I didn't start until now. This is one way I am going to cope with my loss. I want to document the memories I have created the last few days, so I will not lose them.

I begin by sitting in the back room of our house—the "Green Room" we call it. I am listening to my wife Betsy, her sister Emily, and her mother

Kathy grieving upstairs as they move some of Asher's things to his room.

I do not know now how these writings will be organized. They may be stream of consciousness, they may be chronological, or they may be something else entirely. For today, I am going to start chronologically. We'll see how it turns out.

On the morning of April 11, 2016, Betsy called me at school. It was the first day back from Spring Break, and I was preparing for my first class to arrive. Our conversation was brief. She told me that she felt our baby boy flail inside of her and then stop. After the shock of such a movement, she went to the nightstand and pulled out our home Doppler, so she could listen to his heartbeat. She didn't find one. I told her to go into the doctor's office, just in case. If everything was okay, she was going to call me on my cell phone, and I would call her back when I could. If something urgent needed to be communicated to me, she was going to call me on my school phone. I said a silent prayer that everything was okay and continued setting up.

I was hopeful that she was going into labor. Betsy had some signs of preterm labor.

Betsy just finished playing a beautiful medley on the piano. I was sitting, writing, when I heard the first bit of piano since we've been home. I went into the living room to listen. The music included "On Eagle's Wings," "Glory Bound," "Down to the River to Pray," "You Are My Sunshine," and "Asher's Theme." While I sat in a chair and cried, I thought of little. I just felt the music. It was a great comfort. We then returned to the Green Room, where Betsy received some comfort from Newton and Bella, Betsy's parents' dogs. They know of the grief and are here to help.

I had just concluded discussing with my principal the plan for when the baby came, and I needed to leave school. I was hopeful and happy. My first class came and went. I was in my second class of the day when my cell phone rang. I was relieved; Betsy called my cell phone, so I knew that it wasn't urgent. A few minutes later, my school phone rang. My heart sank. My gut told me it wasn't good news.

We talked. Another brief conversation. "He's gone." I couldn't feel anything. I knew what I had to do. Through sobs, she said she was going to stay at the doctor's office until I went to get her. I told my students that I had a family matter and immediately left as a couple of my sixth graders said they were excited that my baby was coming. I walked to the car and got in. I started driving. I had few thoughts. I felt little. It wasn't until I had been driving for nearly 15 minutes that a small tear escaped my eye. I needed to keep it together to be safe. I needed to get to Betsy as soon as possible. I needed to not think.

April 15, 2016

I helped Betsy with a breast pump this morning. It has been hard on her to have her milk start to come in. It pains her to know that the natural way of things is for her to feed her child and continue to give him life—but she can't do that. It almost adds insult to injury. But she's making it through. I knew before that she was strong. I know now that she is even stronger than I could have possibly imagined. We are weak when we need to be, and we have friends and family to support us. But beyond that, we are strong and are facing this together.

Michelle, who photographed Asher while we

were at the hospital, brought over our pictures today. They are beautiful. I can't imagine how hard this would have been without them. Memories may fade, but the pictures will help immensely. He is absolutely perfect in all of them. Betsy doesn't like how she looks in them, but I know the truth. She looks like a new mother—and that is perfect. She is beautiful beyond words.

Ashton, my sister, brought over some freezer dinners last night. We had chicken Alfredo and garlic bread, and it was so comforting. It was the first time since before Monday that I was truly hungry and could taste everything. It's reassuring to have Emily and Kathy with us too. It makes my life feel occupied and full of great family.

Later in the day, Betsy, Kathy, Emily, and I took a stroll around the block with the dogs and decided to walk downtown to get some iced coffee. After the coffee, we stopped at a couple shops including the general store, which is run by a lady who I know from my marching band days. We talked with her for a while, and I remembered that she and her husband went through a similar tragedy in their younger years. It's a small (but very tragic) comfort to know that others have gone through this too and are okay.

Shelby came to visit after the walk. It was so good to see her. It was great for Betsy to share the whole story again. I can imagine that the more she tells it, the more it stays engrained in her memory. Shelby wrote a song for Asher—it was beautiful, moving, and perfect, just like him. It is called "Too Wonderful (Asher's Song)." She made us enchiladas for dinner, and my parents and Brittney, my younger sister, came over for dessert. We shared Asher's pictures with everyone then, and it was moving and relieving to see him again. Many tears were shed.

Before going to bed, Betsy asked me if it felt to me like others were taking parts of our pain and experiencing them for themselves, leaving us a little less to cope with. I told her that I did. I think it's a blessing from above. Others can help us move forward, and we all grow closer because of a connection that we now all share.

April 16, 2016

Today had some "normality" to it that at times was comforting. While going out to get some lunch and return a carpet sample, our car battery died. We needed to call my dad to come help us out and give us a jump. Most people would be upset or angry about this, but it was such a "regular" thing to happen that it made me smile. Life hasn't been normal in so long, it seems. For the universe to treat us like everyone else for a small moment was nice. Before trying to start the car again, Betsy asked Asher in her head for help to start the car. When it didn't work, she said that she almost felt a boy's voice telling her, "Come on, mom. That's not how this works." I couldn't help but chuckle.

Later this evening, we went to see Brittney's work in her first ever art show. It was impressive to see some of the work students had done. We kept an eye out to see if there was anything to purchase to hang in the house, maybe in Asher's room. No luck, but it was nice to get out and support Britt.

Today was the first day that I didn't cry. I am not upset at myself for this. I am finding my own way to grieve, and each day is different. One of the hardest (and easiest) parts of this journey is finding how I need to grieve. I expected so much. So much anguish. So many tears. So little happiness. So little laughter. So much all-consuming grief. I assumed that the only way to begin to move on was to feel everything so acutely that it was unbearable. It turns out that it doesn't have to be that way. I am making it through by appreciating the help, kind words, and sympathies of others. This doesn't mean that I miss him less, remember him less, or love him less for not constantly weeping over this tragic loss of a life and future. It's just how I need to cope.

When people see me, they may think that I am being "so strong." In a way, I agree with them, but not for the reasons that they might think. I am not "so strong" because I am putting on a brave face and doing my best to not outwardly show my constant sadness. I am strong because of others. If my sorrow were a boulder, I would be holding it up, my face to the heavens as I struggle to keep it above my head. But instead of letting me struggle alone, all the people around me help me keep the boulder elevated. I can take a break when I need to, to stretch my arms and weep…and when I lift that boulder again, it is a little easier. The boulder—which is now being held by Betsy, my parents, my sisters, my parents-in-law, my sisters-in-law, my brothers-in-law, my friends, my extended family, my co-workers, and all the others who can feel my pain—will one day erode to a small stone. Still present in my life—in everyone's lives—but so much easier to carry. This is how I know we will make it through.

After what seemed like years and no time at all, I made it to the doctor's office to see Betsy. When I got to the room she was in, I closed the door, and we embraced. We wept. Wept for the loss of our unborn son—his life, his future, his everything. We wept for each other—that Betsy didn't have me with her when it happened, that she felt his last moments of life, that she would need to give birth to an unliving child, that we would be childless parents. We wept for our families—the grandson, nephew, cousin, great-grand-son that no one would ever know. We wept for the world—one less bright, shining star in a world so full of tragedy.

Dr. Esguerra came in soon afterward, and we discussed what was to happen next. We had options, but we ultimately decided a caesarean section was best, as Asher was breach and a natural birth had a high chance of complications. It was also the quick-est option and wouldn't prolong the pregnancy any longer than necessary. After another brief discussion of what happens following the birth, we left to pack for the hospital.

In the car on the way home, Betsy called her mother. The wailing that I could hear from the other end of the line was an unearthly expulsion of pure anguish. It is a sound that I will never be able to for-get.

I called my own mother when we got home. Shock and tears. It was a short conversation that ended with "I love you," but I can remember very little of it.

The news spread to the family through our mothers. It was hard to know that all our closest family was getting some of the worst news they would ever hear. Betsy and I sat on the couch and stared as we waited to leave for the hospital. Time has an annoying habit of being too slow and too fast simultaneously in moments like this. I think of it as no time at all that lasts forever.

We arrived at the hospital around 2:30 p.m. The picture hanging on the door to our room was of a single drop of water on a leaf suspended over a purple background. We would later learn that this symbol, called *The Leaf and the Teardrop*, signifies to all the staff that the room is occupied by someone who has lost their child.

We were taken to our room by a staff member named Cori. I still don't know what her official job title is, but for us, she was someone who we could talk to and ask questions about our situation. I didn't know it yet, but she was one of the most important people I would ever meet.

April 18, 2016

Yesterday was nice but tiring. Andy, Betsy's father, came back to Auburn to get Kathy and the dogs so they could go back home. He spent the morning with us, just chatting and helping a bit around the house. My parents invited us over for an outdoor family day since it was one of the first nice days we've had in a while. It was good to get everyone together again before Andy and Kathy left. We ate burgers and relaxed out on the deck. After we said goodbye to Andy and Kathy, the rest of us played Queens (a card game), and Betsy even decided that she was okay to hold Paisley, our six-month-old niece, for the first time since before Monday.

The weather has been extra sporadic this year, even for Indiana. After a mild winter, it got warm quickly. Just as quickly, it cooled back down and snowed for a few days. Literally a week later, it was in the 70s, and it felt like summer. One good thing about this weather, though, is that it didn't adversely affect the flora around our house. When Shelby visited, she noticed how perfect it was that the two trees outside Asher's windows were in full bloom with white blossoms. Looking around, we also noticed flowers blooming in our landscaping—we didn't even know there were flowers planted there. I like to think all of this is a gift from Asher. The rest of the town is behind—it still looks dead like the winter. Some buds are starting, but none are as beautiful as ours. I am thankful.

Cori went through a similar experience when she lost her daughter Norah back in 2011. Part of her job is to be there for parents who have lost their child since she has first-hand experience. I started to get overwhelmed when she talked about "making memories" and all the other things that we would be able to do with our baby once he was born.

I didn't know what I wanted. At first, I didn't even want to see him. He was gone, and there was nothing that would have brought him back. Why would I want to spend time with the lifeless body of the child I would never raise? They told me that I could see him. Hold him. Touch him. Kiss him. Be with him for as long as we needed while we were in the hospital. Get pictures with him. Bathe him. Baptize him. Read to him. Sing to him. Anything I wanted. I didn't understand. He was gone. I didn't want any of that. It was disturbing to me to think of doing any of that with a body that didn't contain my son's soul.

Cori left and our nurse returned. She described the procedure and answered any questions we had. Nurses came and went for a while, and Betsy and I talked and cried. I asked to talk with Cori again to hear more from someone who had been through this tragedy too.

She came and we talked. I first asked about pictures. How many did she have? "Over 500—and I wish I had 500 more." What should we do with him? "Whatever you want. My husband read parts of *The Hobbit* to Norah." What if I don't want to do any of

15

these things? "Do what you want."

"This is your only time with Asher," she told us. "Make all the memories you can. I recommend doing everything and getting pictures of it all. If you don't do it now, you may regret not doing it later. Get pictures. If you don't want to look at them now, I can guarantee you will want to see them later."

And that's when I knew that she changed my life. I knew that I wanted everything. And there wouldn't be enough time.

***

Today was the hardest day for Betsy so far. It's been hard for me too, but it's been harder for her. This is the first day that we haven't had people staying with us. She woke up and started to feel the finality of what is. It's been great to be surrounded by people to help us through the first stage of our journey. But now we are more alone. So many would flock to us if we said the word, but they aren't here now. We need this time—but it's oh so hard.

We went to John Ley Monuments and ordered an urn. We looked at memorial boxes as well—granite boxes that remain above ground like a tombstone, though Asher will not be buried. The boxes weren't exactly what we were looking for, as they were made for ashes. Hopefully, they can make something that would be ideal for us. The urn should be here in the next few days, so we can see if it's exactly what we want.

Later we went to Fort Wayne. At Costco, we browsed patio furniture that would allow us to sit and enjoy being with Asher in our garden. We decided on a swing that will be perfect. It can be a Mother's Day present to Betsy. I know we will use it a lot. We also went to the Olive Garden for dinner and went to the local arts store for some colored pencils and supplies.

Betsy wanted the pencils to color in her mandala coloring book to help bring her peace. She will probably bring it with her and use it when we leave tomorrow, too. We decided to take a trip to Michigan to get away and have some "us time." We want to be away from people and places we know to give us some time on our own and to make some happy memories, though we are grieving. I look forward to being together—just us.

April 21, 2016

We got back from our trip to Michigan last night. It was perfect timing, and it turned out to be just what we needed. We journeyed to be somewhere away from people who knew we were grieving. That sounds harsh, but it really isn't. It's tiring to be around people who treat you a little bit differently and are grieving too. Don't get me wrong—the love and support that we've gotten has been wonderful and healing. But it's still tiring. We needed some alone time to grieve together and do something that made us happy. For us, travel answered both of those needs.

Before we left, Betsy mentioned that she felt that we needed to go on this trip in order to find something important. Her intuition with this kind of thing is usually spot on. She was, of course, right on target.

We headed to Frankenmuth, Michigan on Tuesday morning. I had been there once before and knew there was some good food and interesting shopping there. We first went to Bronner's, the world's largest Christmas store, to check out the nutcrackers (I collect them). I thought that maybe an angel nutcracker would be what Betsy felt we were going to find. Unfortunately, we had no such luck. We did have a nice time there and left with a beautiful ornament for Asher with his name on it. We bought a stand for it as well, so it won't only be hanging on the Christmas tree—it will have a place of its own year round.

After indulging in a great meal, interesting local beer from the Frankenmuth Brewery, and two pounds of fudge, we continued our journey toward Traverse City. We didn't decide on what we were going to do or even where to stay that night until we got to the city. We got a room at the Best Western and took a cat nap to rest after the long drive. Betsy looked up some info about what to do in the area, and we decided to go to a meadery before hitting the sack.

The meadery was called the Acoustic Taphouse. This location gave us exactly what we as a grieving couple needed—good booze and an experience we will never forget. As we looked at the menu of meads and ciders that they offered online, we knew that we wanted to try everything because it all sounded amazing. But when we pulled up, the first thing I said was, "Are we going to get mugged?" This building was the definition of a "hole in the wall." It very well may have been the smallest building in the city. There was NO WAY that this rinky-dink bar could serve good drinks.

We went in anyway. The atmosphere was not at all what we expected. The tiny room had a small bar and a couple tables. There were instruments everywhere. Literally everywhere. In one corner of the room (I had to push past one of them just to get in the door) were two guys playing guitar and singing. Two things were immediately obvious—they were drunk, and they were high. Surprisingly, their music wasn't bad—granted, it was hard to understand them. The bartender—a young guy, maybe a year or two younger than me—told us about his meads and ciders, and we decided to try them all. He brought us flights of the amber and pink liquids in old, cheap ukuleles with holes drilled in them. They were all fantastic. So fantastic, in fact, that we paid *way* too much to leave with a case of their raspberry jasmine mead.

We stayed for about an hour and watched, listened, drank, and talked. It may not sound that interesting, but it's a night I know Betsy and I will never forget. After stopping for some ice cream, we went back to our hotel and watched some Netflix before going to sleep.

Wednesday was filled with shopping, drinking wine, and admiring the cherry-flavored everything. We spent some time in downtown Traverse City doing some shopping. My personal favorite was the shop full of anything that you could dream of that had to do with cherries. Betsy found a nice dress, and we looked in a lot of shops until we found the thing for which we were meant to come to Traverse City.

The art gallery was called Art & Soul. We went in just for fun, but it turned into so much more. The gallery was small, and we started to walk around the perimeter of the room. Along the back wall were some of the most vibrant paintings I have ever seen. They were beautiful pictures of nature in colors that I wouldn't have imagined. They were stunning. We looked at each and every piece painted by G. Peebles. We knew early on that we needed one of the pieces to hang over our fireplace in remembrance of Asher. Many of his pieces were lone trees—ash trees. They were painted in vibrant colors of orange, red, blue, green, and purple that made the trees come alive in a way that is impossible on Earth.

When talking with the proprietor of the gallery about George Peebles, we learned that he was, in fact, colorblind and he painted everything based on memory and his emotions. He truly spoke to us through his work.

Unfortunately, the pieces that the gallery had were not exactly what we were looking for—the few that we thought were perfect for us were either too big or too small. We found out that he does commission works, though, for the same price we would have paid in the gallery. We received his contact information and are going to communicate with him soon to have Asher's masterpiece commissioned. It will be perfect.

Through this beginning part of our journey without Asher, we have had a tremendous amount of support both emotionally and financially. A friend from college, Leah Kincaid, started a GoFundMe page in Asher's memory. We have been abundantly blessed by our friends, family, and anonymous donors to have raised enough money to cover our medical expenses and all memorials that we want for Asher. The painting, the perfect tribute to our little angel, would not be possible without the financial support of those who care about Asher and us. Betsy and I are forever humbled by the generosity shown to us, and we are eternally grateful.

As if we weren't already positive that this trip was what we needed, the universe decided to throw us another curveball and prove that we were where we were supposed to be. Our final stop before heading back to Indiana was a small, new winery on the peninsula. When we walked in, there were about eight people in the room. One of them was a teacher from the school in Chicago where I taught last year. There is no way that coincidence could lead us to the same tiny winery on the Traverse Bay peninsula in the middle of April. Catching up with her and her husband was a great way to show us that we were ready to go back to the people we knew and loved.

Throughout our trip, we talked of Asher. We talked of who he could have been. We talked of our grief. We talked about "what happens next." But unlike most times in the past, we talked with a bit more happiness. Because of where we were and the nature of our visit, we could, for a brief moment, move past the very present anguish we were feeling and get a taste of what acceptance and contentment feel like. I hope some of this feeling remains.

April 22, 2016

My mom and I went to Fort Wayne to see Barry Manilow in concert tonight. We lucked out and got some comp tickets from some friends at Heartland Sings (a local professional singing group that Betsy used to sing with) who sang backup for him on a couple songs. Barry was *amazing*.

It was really great to hang out with my mom as Betsy spent time with my siblings at home eating up leftovers from all of the food people brought us. Getting back to normality a little bit at a time.

We also received money from a food fundraiser

my dad had at his work. His company provided hot dogs to the workers for a freewill donation. It really shows how much people love my dad—they raised $1,000. Betsy and I are overjoyed and humbled by this generosity.

April 23, 2016

Today was a good day for a number of reasons: the weather was beautiful, we got Asher's remains back with us, and the inevitable happened—we got a dog (at least temporarily).

We got up this morning to pick up Asher's filled urn and death certificate—I find it a little disconcerting and disrespectful that Asher did not receive a birth certificate too, but I digress. His urn is the one we picked out at John Ley Monuments. It's white marble with gray streaks in it. Very hefty and quite beautiful. It's good to have him back with us. We placed him on top of the piano, so he can always be close to our music. I am grateful that my mom had the idea to have Asher cremated. Now, he will always be with us. If we ever move homes, he will be close.

After the funeral home, Betsy wanted to go to the Noble County Humane Shelter to look at dogs. I was originally against it, but we decided that we would go just to look. If we liked one in particular, maybe we would fill out an application after we seriously talked about it. As we had this discussion, I—always the pragmatist—brought up the expenses, time, and energy that would go into dog ownership.

I knew that getting a dog wasn't just "filling the baby void" for Betsy. She's wanted one for so long, but it just didn't work with our lifestyle. Now things are different. Betsy's arguments are more valid and convincing: she wanted something to take care of (besides our cat), she wasn't working and thus had time, and she craved the joy a dog brings to a household. I eventually agreed that it may be a possibility, but *only* if we fell in love with the perfect one.

We went to the shelter and looked at a few dogs that Betsy was interested in. They were lovable, high-energy, cute, and (sometimes) cat-friendly. Unfortunately, none of them gave me the "spark" I was looking for in a companion. We went home to put Asher's remains in the house and get some lunch.

Betsy wanted to go to the DeKalb County Humane Society, too, since she was hoping to volunteer there now that she had the time. We pulled up and went to look at some more dogs. We got a little closer this time—we found some strong potential candidates. But again, no "spark." Perhaps if we took some time, I would come around and realize that I did fall in love with one of them. We were asked to fill out an application anyway so that when we did find the perfect pet, we would be on the "fast track" to adoption.

We were going to take the application home, but the Assistant Director convinced us that we could fill it out in the cat room and get to play with some cats before we left. We conceded. As we were walking back, she said, "Well, you could come in here and sit with a Dachshund instead." Well, that was a no-brainer. Cats are cool, but dachshunds are better. We went in and the "spark" filled my chest.

The poor little guy was brought into the shelter at 2 a.m. with ticks and a neck wound. He was shaken up but so cute and in need of some love. We could help with that. We spent some time with him and we found out that he needed a foster home ASAP. Because of his wound, he couldn't stay in the shelter for another night. The AD asked if we would be interested. We, of course, said yes.

The application process normally takes three to four days, but because the AD had a good feeling about us, she said she could accept us right away. Betsy decided that it was an okay time to tell her the story of Asher; she explained that we had recently lost our son and needed someone to take care of and love. The AD commenced through tears to tell us of her 19-year-old daughter, who was her whole world. She couldn't imagine living without her. She had lost her husband many years ago and therefore knows the hurt of losing someone so dear. She said that God was blessing us by bringing us together with this dog. We felt the same way. We're not sure if it was God, the Holy Spirit, or even Asher himself who led us together, but we were a perfect match.

We left soon afterward with our foster puppy, who we decided to name Leonardo (Leo for short) after da Vinci. If his owners claim him within five days, he will return to them. After that, he is up for adoption. As his foster parents, we have first rights to adopt him. If we decide we don't want to adopt him, he will stay with us until a suitable home has been found for him.

Based on today, I think he'll stay with us. He's cuddly, friendly, gets along with our cat, and is exactly what we need. Hopefully, Leo will be with us for a long time.

As I'm sure you've noticed, I haven't continued the story of the hospital in a few days. I have been putting it off, but I am afraid that if I keep putting it off, my memory will start to fade. I will try to be more vigilant.

The next few hours went so slowly yet flew by. Looking back, it was no time at all, but it seemed to drag on and on. We were told the plan for the C-section and what was to follow. Because our time with him would be so short, the nurses offered to take as many pictures as they could.

5:30 p.m. rolled around, and it was time for Betsy to leave for the epidural. I followed the team of doctors and nurses down the hall to the operating room, and I stayed in the recovery room until they were ready for the delivery.

While I waited, I sat there and sobbed. This was

the first time that I had to myself to truly process what was happening. My son was gone. My beloved child who I didn't even get the chance to meet in this world was gone—and he was never coming back. I questioned God. I felt pain in my chest. I let all my emotion roll down my cheeks. And I waited.

A few people came to see me in that room. I could compose myself (almost) before they came by. I saw one of the nurses, who gave her condolences. I met the photographer who would later play a great role in the time my son was with us. Dr. Esguerra came in to give me a genuine hug and tell me he would take care of Betsy. And Cori came to see me. She was, yet again, a great comfort. Just to know that someone else had gone through this unbearable anguish was a comfort. She made it through. And so would Betsy and I.

I was ushered in to sit with Betsy as they delivered our baby. She was in pain from an intense headache but could feel nothing below her breasts. I rubbed her temples to help her relax. We talked briefly and listened to the music playing. While waiting in the recovery room, Dr. Esguerra asked me if it was okay if he listened to some Christian music while he operated. I told him that Betsy probably wouldn't mind, but he should ask her. Evidently, she recommended the Melody Gardot Pandora station, as it was playing some familiar old vocal jazz tunes.

At 6:14 p.m., Asher Joseph Ley was brought into this world. I got to see him first. He was the most beautiful thing I had ever seen. I heard the doctor and nurses exchange some jargon including confirmation that there was no heartbeat. "Baby I'm a Fool" by Melody Gardot played in the background. My emotions were on the most intense roller coaster that has ever existed. There was my son. *My* son. My only child. I was so happy to finally see him. But he wasn't my son. My son had already passed on. What I was seeing were just his earthly remains. My heart and soul ached for him. For Betsy. For me. He would never grow older than he was at that exact moment. He would forever be immortalized in my mind as the perfect baby. I still don't know how I feel about that; it gives me a strange mixture of joy, anguish, and love. My heart ached (and still does) from how much love I have for the son I will never raise.

April 24, 2016

I went over to where he was laid to see him. There he was. My baby boy. Sprawled out and naked for the whole world to see. He looked even more perfect than I could have hoped. As soon as they were done with the initial postpartum steps, they handed him to me and I held my son for the first time. I cried. I can still feel his weight in my arms and see his tiny body that wouldn't move on its own. I brought him over to Betsy, so she could see the tragic miracle in my arms.

I sat and she lay there for a few minutes as we both cried out of joy for seeing him and sadness for knowing that our time together was already too short. I passed him to her, and she held him on her chest for a while. I stroked her hair and tried to bring some comfort to both of us as the hospital staff stitched Betsy back up behind the curtain.

We were in the recovery room for a few hours following. I don't know what compelled her to ask, but our nurse, Nicole, asked me if I wanted to measure him. I was happy to do so. 17.5 inches long; head, 13 inches; chest, 10.75 inches. A little later, I asked if fathers usually got to measure or if this was just something special for the fathers of angels. She told me that I was the first father she'd ever let measure. I was honored and thankful for that moment with my boy.

Michelle Glenn, a volunteer photographer with Now I Lay Me Down to Sleep (a non-profit organization who introduces remembrance photography to parents suffering the loss of a baby), came into the room to capture our moments together with Asher. She would stay with us for much of the time that we had Asher with us. I cannot thank her enough for her services in preserving our time together in beautiful photographs. She took perfect pictures that conveyed everything we were feeling and immortalized moments we never wanted to forget.

We spent this time looking at him. We looked at his eyes—blue, like mine and my mother's (we were told that it was the kind of blue that would stay blue). We looked at his ears—rounded, like Betsy's. We looked at his legs—long, like his Aunt Emily's. We looked at his mouth—shaped just like his mommy's. We looked at his arms hairs—they swirled just like his daddy's. We looked at his hair—copper like his grandpa's. We looked at his toes and fingers—long and delicate like Betsy's (great fingers for piano playing). He was perfect.

This morning, I went back to church for the first time since Asher's passing. Betsy stayed home since she needed to look after Leo, but I still wanted to go with my mom. It was harder than I thought to be there, not because of the church aspect of it, but because of the families. I saw three families with more than four kids each. The kids were rowdy and disruptive, and their parents were having a hard time keeping them in their seats. All that I could think was, "I would love to have that problem right now." Church was also challenging because I had time to think and reflect. Reflecting and tears are good, but not in the middle of a church service.

We took Leo to PetSmart later, and we stopped at Costco to get Betsy's Mother's Day present: the outdoor swing. On the way home, Betsy and I got into a bit of an argument that we resolved. One thing that I will say about us as people and as a married couple is that we have no problem communicating. Sometimes miscommunication happens, but it gets resolved through more talking. I don't think we could have made it through this without being able to communicate with each other so well.

Kathy came back today with Newton and Bella. They get along just fine with Leo. It will be good to have Kathy here with Betsy when I go back to work tomorrow. I'm not looking forward to being away but going back to work is a necessary step. Now is as good a time as any.

April 25, 2016

I went back to school today. I didn't think it would be a good day. It was the first time Betsy and I would be spending the day apart since we lost Asher, but it needed to be done.

It turns out that I was wrong. Because it was a professional development day, I got a chance to see all my colleagues without having kids everywhere. This gave them an opportunity to share their sympathies and talk easily. It was really nice getting to see everyone again after a month and resume "real life." My old theater director shared with me that his wife and he lost a child too. They went through ten miscarriages then lost a daughter after having her for five days. They finally had another daughter a year later—their one and only child—and they are so thankful for her. He gave me a hug and reassured me that next time we have a child, everything will be okay. It meant a lot to me.

Before the meeting with the other teachers at my school, I made an announcement to let them know that I am open to talking about Asher if anyone had any questions or anything. I could see tension leave some people's faces as if they had been hoping to hear just that. Some of them did have questions that I was happy to answer. I am happy to share his story and pictures with anyone who wants to know about my son.

We went back to our room and continued to spend time with our baby. We gave Betsy a little bit more time to rest before I went out to get her parents, who had driven in from Ohio. I greeted them outside the room, and we hugged and cried. I braced them for the fact that Asher was in the room. If they didn't want to see him, that was okay. They did want to see him.

39

Betsy was holding him when they came in, and they came over to hug Betsy and look at their first grandchild. The pure emotion in the room was tangible. Everyone sobbed unrelentingly. When Andy and Kathy held him, it was one of the most devastating sights I've ever seen. If it were a painting, it would be called "The Loss of a Grandchild." It was a powerful thing to see.

The next part of our stay (like others to come) was a blur of sadness and attempts at normal conversation. Asher was passed between us and his Oma and Grandy. It was obvious how much they love him. We found out that Abby, Betsy's sister, was flying into Chicago from San Francisco so she and Emily could drive over together.

More time passed, and my parents and Brittney came. I met them outside the room too, and I embraced each of them for a long time. When I gave them the option of seeing him, they all wanted to meet our angel. Andy and Kathy stepped out to give them some time with us.

It was even more heartbreaking for me this time since it was my immediate family. When my mom held him, all I could think was, "My poor mother." My dad held him, and it hurt me physically to see such anguish in his eyes. Brittney held her nephew and sobbed for the boy she wouldn't know as he grew older. More tears ensued. I thought, "Is it possible for me to cry any more today?"

Betsy's family came back in after a while, and Ashton joined a little later than that. She was unable to find someone to watch Paisley, so she had her with her. She was worried that Paisley would be a problem because we just lost a child—Paisley was only six months old. She came in, and I felt joy to see Paisley. I had happy memories with her. It helped that she was older, that she was a girl, that she was my niece, and she was quiet. Those things helped keep me from thinking even more about what we lost with Asher. It was a little harder for Betsy, but she did just fine. Ashton had her moment to hold Asher too. It was hard for her because she lamented how much he looked like Paisley. Her heart broke like everyone else's.

Our support team was growing. The nurses were there for Betsy and me. Betsy and I were there for our families. Our families were there for each other and us. And we were all there for Asher.

April 27, 2016

After school today, Cori—the librarian at my school—came into my room to talk with me. She expressed her sympathies in person about the loss of Asher. But as the conversation continued, it turned out that the conversation wasn't just for me, but for her too.

As it turned out, she had six different pregnancies, but she only had three children. She miscarried three times. In addition to those losses, she lost her boyfriend to a car accident many years ago. They were planning on moving in together and starting their own journey in life. He was taken from her too soon.

She shared her feelings of loss as I had shared mine. While it is different for each person in different situations, losing someone you love is always painful and never really leaves you. Here is one of the most impactful things she shared with me:

"I hated hearing, 'Why do bad things always happen to good people?' It made me mad that I felt like I was a good person, but these terrible things happened anyway. But now I think I understand why. Bad things happen to good people because good people can make a difference. Your story has helped me get over some of the anger that I've been holding in for so long."

Losing my son was unbearable, but it touched many people, and that means a lot to me. Both Betsy and I have shared our experience with others as a coping mechanism. Non-person-to-person communication has primarily been done on social media and Betsy's blog. Our story has helped many people already. They have come forward to let us know how we helped them in some way. I can only hope that we have helped others too, in ways they have not expressed.

This evening we went to go visit Grandma Ley in the nursing home. Her health is declining as the

Parkinson's takes over. She was taken to the hospital a few days ago and was brought to Sacred Heart Home for physical therapy and other rehab. I don't expect she will leave. It was good to see her, but hard, as she wasn't making much sense when we talked with her. I pray that when the time is right, God will take her home. Maybe Grandpa Ley and Asher will be there to guide her.

April 28, 2016

Later in the evening, we decided that it was time to give him his first (and only) bath. Normally, the nursing staff takes care of that a few hours or so after birth, but in our case, they told us that we could do it ourselves whenever we wanted to. They brought in a small bowl of warm water and some small washcloths.

Betsy and I took our time. We cleaned him the best we could while being extra careful. If we washed too hard, it might have caused damage to his skin. Betsy took her time ensuring that every inch of him was washed, while I followed up with a dry towel. She started with his feet—they were so tiny—and moved her way up. His head was the most difficult to clean, I think. The last thing we wanted was to scrub too hard and accidentally remove some of his hair. It was so soft afterward.

The nurses took our clean baby over to the bed where he would stay the night. After getting his footprints (as many as we wanted), they wrapped him up and began to take pictures. I am so happy that they did this for us. They put him in a couple different outfits and got some adorable pictures with him and the teddy bear the hospital gave him.

They also took some pictures of him with the ceramic hearts they gave to us. There were three separate pieces: a small square piece that had a heart carved in it, a small heart-shaped piece, and a larger heart necklace that the small heart fit into. They told us that the square piece went to me, the necklace went to Betsy, and the small heart went to Asher when we buried him. It symbolized him always having a piece of our hearts with him. I knew then that my heart would never be completely whole again. It would always have a small part left open for Asher.

May 1, 2016

Friday was a hard day for Betsy. Possibly the hardest day for her since the hospital. Kathy left in the morning, and as soon as she was gone, Betsy lost many of her "distractions."

She sent me a text that just said, "Today is a rough day." When I asked her what specifically was wrong, she said, "The numbness has worn away, and now I just feel ripped wide open. I want my son back. I don't want to look at other people's babies because mine is gone. I'm a mother with no child, and I feel so displaced and alone." I wanted to leave school then. I needed to be home with her. Unfortunately, I needed to finish my day at work.

I was on the volunteer list for the school carnival that night, but I thought it would be best for us if I stayed home so we could have an evening together. We decided to go out to dinner and stay in to watch a movie. We got some wine and moved the TV up to the bedroom, where we spent a nice candlelit evening together.

Shelby and Isaac came over last night. It was really great to see them and have a nice, normal evening with friends, but it was bittersweet at the same time. Betsy described it well when she said that it was weird to have a "normal" night. We barely even mentioned Asher. We could pretend we were the people that we used to be or (perhaps more accurately) the people we are going to be after some time has passed. Perhaps someday soon we will be in the mood to go to a cookout, a baseball game, or dinner with friends and feel okay about being "normal." Only time will tell.

Soon after his photos were taken, we requested that a minister come in to give him a baptism. It was short and moving, and I am happy that we made this decision. Even though Asher's soul has already departed, it felt right to give his body the sacrament. We were even able to keep his baptismal water with us to bring home.

Following the ceremony, all of us clasped hands—my parents, Brittney, Betsy's parents, the minister, and me—and gathered around Betsy's bed, where she held our newly christened son. The minister said a prayer, and Andy asked to say one as well. I no longer remember exactly what was said by them, but it was moving and touching. It was exactly what Asher deserved.

Our families left shortly after, and Betsy and I were left alone with our baby as we began a very difficult night. We would have given anything to have the same challenging night that most parents face—the first night of crying and fussing and really feeling like parents. Instead, ours was full of silence and sorrow.

I took Asher over to his bed, which had been lined with a cooling pack (called a Cuddle Cot) that helped his body keep its color and not turn purple. I went to the couch and pulled it out into a bed. Betsy remained in her semi-upright position and tried to sleep. Luckily/unluckily I fell asleep easily. It was a long, hard day, and I needed some rest. The bad parts were my dreams. I don't remember them exactly, and I wouldn't have called them "nightmares," but they were not pleasant.

In the middle of the night, I woke up to hear Betsy and our nurse, Leah, talking. I am thankful for Leah that night. She told Betsy before she went to sleep that Betsy was her only charge that night. She told her to call for anything, even if it was just for someone to talk to or to sit at her bedside in silence. Leah was there for us both—to comfort Betsy and to give me my needed rest.

I don't know when Betsy called her in, but they stayed up for a few hours talking about their lives. I was awake for the bit about how Betsy and I met and where I was from. It turned out that Leah's fiancé and I graduated from the same high school. I didn't know him personally, but I knew his older brother. In fact, his older brother is married to my cousin. Leah was going to be my cousin's sister-in-law in just a few short months. It's a small world.

I can't speak for Betsy, but I hope we meet Leah again one day—perhaps when we have our next child. I am so happy that she was there for Betsy. She was a gift for us both that night. She was also the one who took some of Asher's pictures. She's a bigger part of his story than she knows.

Before going to sleep, I checked Facebook once more to find that Kathy wrote a gorgeous poem:

A Tribute to a Special Mother

A woman becomes a mother from the
  moment she opens up her heart.
To the thought of loving and caring for a
  child, it is the start.
But sometimes she finds there are other
  plans,
And that little one is swept from her loving
  hands.
Yet love binds them together even though
  they are apart.
In her mind's eye, she sees her little boy with
  strawberry-blond curls,
Singing loudly and dancing with spins and
  great twirls.
He is holding the hands of another's girl
  child.

Their friendship is sweet, though their
    movements are wild.
His mother treasures this thought in her
    heart like precious pearls.
We humans are a fragile lot,
Our lives a vapor, first here, and then not.
Asher's mother longs and awaits the day,
When she will hold him close and watch him
    play,
Where the light of God's love is more than
    mere thought.

May 3, 2016

Our days are still hard. Betsy and I are often called to act like everything hasn't changed, and that's the biggest challenge of all. So often when I am at school, I need to push down my grief and thoughts of Asher, so my students aren't aware of my melancholy. Over the last week or so, I've gotten used to this feeling, and it's started to become more natural. This frightens me. I do not want to be a pretender, but that is what my profession requires. I don't want to be good at it; I want to show my feelings when I need to and not put on a mask for my students' sake. But alas, things are not that simple.

Betsy is not ready for things to go back to "normal." She does not and will not pretend. She has not been forced into a situation yet that causes her to mask her emotions like I have. I envy her because she does not have to pretend. I do not envy her because I feel the day is coming when she is going to have to—especially when she returns to the workforce. She does not have a job now, but we both know that she will need one in a couple of months to help bring in income. She's not looking forward to that day, and neither am I. I just pray that she will be in a better place when the time comes so the transition is not too hard.

Betsy and I went to a Bernie Sanders rally yesterday. It was a lot of fun and definitely worth the wait. I saw my best friend Jamie there for the first time since before we lost Asher. It was great to see him, but I wish we had met up sooner. I wanted our first meeting to be a time when I could talk to him about my son. I haven't had that time with one of my close friends yet, and I would still like to. We need to get together so I have another person to share his story with.

On a happy note, I accepted the open band director position at the middle school yesterday. This is a step in the right direction. It will be hard for me to leave my new friends at North Side and South Side, but this is the best decision for me right now. I will never be able to thank them enough for their willingness to bring me into their family at school. They were there for me during this hard time too, and they will never know how much that meant to me.

May 6, 2016

L ast night was my first night back to community band since we went to the hospital. It was an odd experience for me, but not for the reasons that I thought it would be.

The whole day I felt strange. Normally, I don't drink coffee, but there was some free coffee in the teachers' lounge for Teacher Appreciation Week. I regretted drinking it because the caffeine usually causes me to feel apprehensive, like I was anticipating an event that I was not looking forward to. Beyond that, my stomach just felt weird. I had a small feeling that I needed some Asher time that day. I asked Betsy if we could reminisce in the hopes that it would make me feel better and she agreed. Due to some schedule changes, though, that never happened, and I went straight to band.

When I got there, I realized immediately what was wrong. No one there knew that I was a different person. Nobody asked me how I was doing or extended their sympathies. It wasn't that I needed those things, but I needed to know that they *knew*. But they didn't. During the whole rehearsal they treated me like I was the same person—I am not that person anymore. I longed for someone to ask me where I had been for the last few weeks, so I could share Asher with them. Those questions never came.

Afterward, I stayed and talked with Adam. This was exactly what I needed. This interaction was what I had been anticipating all day, but it wasn't the negative event I thought it would be. I just needed to share. I needed to share the whole story.

After some small talk, Adam and I talked about Asher. He asked questions, I gave answers, and I told Asher's story. The whole story. I cried for the first time in many days. It was healing.

I felt so much better today after talking to Adam last night. My day was just fine. When I came home,

Betsy and I did some cleaning to get ready for her friend Richelle to visit. Her visit gave Betsy the opportunity to share like I shared with Adam. It was healing for us both.

May 8, 2016

Betsy's first Mother's Day was a hard one. After many tears this morning, we decided not to go to church. We haven't been back since we lost Asher, but we thought that maybe today we could return. In the end, Betsy didn't feel that she would be able to make it through and keep her composure.

We spent the morning talking and grieving. Then, after preparing the cheese potatoes to take to my parents' house (we were going there for dinner) and walking Leo, we visited Fort Wayne to shop for a new board game. We ended up buying one before heading to Avilla, where my parents live.

I was glad that we got to spend some time with the family, especially my mom, on Mother's Day. The weather was nice, and we had some delicious BBQ chicken wings. We made it through okay, but it's still kind of hard to see Paisley with Ashton and Ryne. It's not because she reminds us of Asher or that we can't be around babies, but instead because both Betsy and I wish that we could have a child to look at us like she looks at her parents. You can see that they love her deeply and she lights up when she sees them. It's exactly how a child/parent relationship should be—we just wish we had that too.

I want to leave this entry with the poem Betsy wrote on Friday:

My mind asks,
"What do you know of love?"
My heart replies…
His eyes are truest blue
As calming and soothing as evening prayer
Yet as vivid and mysterious as the Northern
    Lights
What do I know of love?
His skin is softest velvet

In all the world, my lips have never kissed
    anything so sweet
Joyfully, hungrily—they seek every inch of
    him
His hair is finest curls
In a color only heaven can dye
Perfectly encircling his head
What do I know of love?
Though he walks in blissful perfection
He will never be mine to hold
What do I know of love?
I know that love can be taken away
Only just after meeting
After the spell has struck
And you are fated to feeling, to care
What do I know of love?
I know that while he is gone
My heart will cling to him
As one clings to their own life
As tightly and intimately as lovers hold each
    other in the night
I have knit him so certainly on my heart
That not one day will pass when it will not
    remember his presence there
What do I know of love?

I know his name.
I know his name.
I know his name.
His name is Asher!

May 9, 2016

Our insurance may not be working like we hoped it would. Because my job required Betsy to be covered under her own insurance policy if her job offered one, she was covered under two different policies. This was fine until we realized that we would be paying into two deductibles.

The original plan was for Betsy to finish working before the baby was born. She was supposed to be off her insurance by April 18. We went to the hospital on April 11. Her technical last day working was April 9, but she wasn't officially terminated until April 18. This means that she was still covered under her insurance when we went in for her C-section, which means we will need to pay into her deductible (a substantial one) and mine. That's an extra $6,500 that we weren't planning on paying.

I've been in contact with my HR rep at school and the business manager at Betsy's former workplace trying to figure this out, so we only have to pay my deductible. This is very stressful for both Betsy and me. We can't afford to have that extra payment into an insurance plan that she's not even covered under anymore. I hope they get back to me with good news.

We had planned for this. We had planned for her to be done before she went into labor. But life had other plans. Why did we (Betsy especially) need to go through surgery, pain, grief, and come out with a dead son and, on top of it all, need to pay a large amount of money? Why is this happening? How could life be so cruel? It was bad enough to lose the son who we were so excited to have. Why must we now PAY for nothing? I don't know what we'll do if this happens.

<hr />

The next morning was a shock. Less than twenty-four hours ago we had a living son in my wife's womb ready to be loved and raised. Then he was gone.

Betsy and I spent the morning talking (barely) and being with Asher because we knew we had such little time left with him. I ordered breakfast, but it was hard to eat. I wasn't hungry, and what I did eat had no taste. Never before had strong emotions robbed me of my sense of taste. I hope I never have to experience that again.

Grief made the time pass annoyingly slowly, yet very quickly. In the late morning, my in-laws arrived and spent some time with Asher, Betsy, and me. Soon after that, Betsy's sisters, Abby and Emily, came too. Abby flew to Chicago from San Francisco, and she and Emily drove in together. The mourning and agony came flooding back. It was hard for Betsy and me to know that Asher had been lost and to hold his lifeless body, but it wasn't as painful after a little bit of "getting used to it." But every time someone new came in to see him and experience his loss, a wound reopened in my soul.

They held him and sobbed. We each embraced and gave each other comfort. It was around this time that I realized how much physical pain I was in. You hear that heartbreak hurts, but I always thought it was in a figurative or emotional sense. But, no. Heartbreak quite literally sent a deep ache through my chest. I still feel that way sometimes, but not as often anymore.

We all got caught up on each other's lives. It was then that the unthinkable happened: we laughed. Everyone started exchanging stories, and some funny ones came up. It seemed that we would never laugh again, but it came. It came naturally—not forced at all. I believe to this day that Asher helped lift our spirits enough to experience some joy while he was with us. We have a picture of Andy holding Asher while everyone in the room was laughing. This is how I want to remember Asher's time with us.

Two days ago, we got the *great* news that our insurance went through. They back-dated Betsy's termination to her last day of work, so we will only have to pay into my deductible. PRAISE THE LORD.

Yesterday marked one month since Asher's death. Betsy and I both felt bad that neither of us even realized it until someone pointed it out over the phone. It's understandable, though, since he is such a large part of our lives now. We think about him for a lot of the day and talk about him often. It wasn't a huge shock because nothing has really changed. Yesterday was just another day. Another day on our new path.

To commemorate him, we decided that we should have a nice day. No sadness or tears. Just happiness and good times. I took the day off work, and we played games, laughed, and spent some time with friends. Betsy even took a relaxing bath. It was a good day.

A little bit later in the day, Michelle, the photographer, came back to the hospital to get some more pictures. While she took some shots of his footprints, we all continued our visit together. We shared more stories and talked of normal things. Occasionally, the talk turned to Asher. But, surprisingly, it wasn't always sad. Sometimes we discussed more lighthearted topics, like which family members he resembled. Other times, though, we talked longingly of the future he wouldn't have and shed some tears.

At different times during the day, I made calls to friends who we felt should know that we had lost him. Shelby had planned a baby shower for Betsy on the upcoming Saturday, so I needed to call her to cancel it. I also called my closest friends—Tyler, Adam, Curtis, Jamie, Blake, Chris, and Sara—to let them know. Most of them I got to right away, but others I needed to talk to later. They were all as supportive as they could have been. All their offers to talk or help in any way were much appreciated. I love them all for being there for me.

At some point in the day, I don't quite remember when, Emily and I had a moment together that brought us closer. She was sitting on the couch by herself crying—again, I don't remember why—while we all cried too. I could see that she needed some comfort, so I walked over to the couch and sat with her. I put an arm around her and gave her any comfort I could. She leaned into my embrace and cried on my shoulder. She would later return the favor the night we got home, when we told Betsy's mom and sisters how we said goodbye to Asher.

While we had the photographer, we wanted to get pictures of Asher in various outfits. The handmade items were most important; they included a hat from my Aunt Glenda. The hospital also donated an outfit and hat, which had been handmade by a mother for her angel son Harrison. I will probably never meet the woman who made the little white hat, but it fit Asher perfectly, and it made him even more handsome.

We have some pictures too of Asher in a "cocoon" that Kathy made for him. She knitted a cocoon and hat based on the book *The Very Hungry Caterpillar*. The pictures are absolutely adorable. Because of this, the symbol of a butterfly has taken on great significance for Kathy. She has a butterfly on her necklace for him, and she has been folding origami butterflies for him as a coping mechanism. The butterfly is very special, indeed.

Because this was the last time that Michelle would be with us, Betsy's family got final pictures with Asher. The room once again became somber. Even though this wasn't yet goodbye, they knew that these pictures were the last that they were going to have with Asher. My heart still breaks when I look at the pictures.

Michelle got some more of Betsy and me with him too, including my personal favorite—a picture of me holding him while light pours in from the window behind us. Michelle captured some close-ups of each of us with him and some special ones of him with our wedding rings and him wearing his ankle bracelet.

Soon after, my family came because they wanted

pictures as well. My heart shattered, the wound opening yet again. Everyone got some final pictures holding him, except for Ashton. It was too hard for her today because of his resemblance to Paisley. Although she didn't get a picture, I know that the memory of holding him in her arms will be with her forever, just like it is for the rest of us.

Michelle left. We would take no more pictures of our one and only child. We have over 500 pictures, and I would give almost anything to have more.

May 16, 2016

Today is Asher's due date. I feel melancholy, and I wish I could be home to be with Betsy, but there are some important things that I need to do at school today, and I don't have any more personal days to use. I pray that she will find some peace throughout the day. We've had messages from family members saying that they are thinking of Asher and us today. While it's nice to know this, I almost wish they hadn't said anything. Knowing that others are grieving today too is not a comfort. I hope to find a way to honor him today by doing something to bring myself and others joy.

Aunt Wendy was over last Friday to help Betsy with our garden. The two of them did a lot of work and planning; they have some great ideas for around the house to make everything look beautiful. They also spent a lot of time discussing the area of the garden where Asher's things will be. Besides the flowers and plants that will be back there, the area will include:

- A stone that my parents got us. Inscribed on it are the words, "An angel in the book of life wrote down my baby's birth. Then whispered as she closed the book 'too beautiful for Earth.'"

- The wind chimes that my parents-in-law got us. We don't have this yet, but it will be coming to us soon. The pitches of the chimes are taken from "Asher's Theme," a piano piece Betsy wrote for him.

- A small baby angel statue from Shelby and Stephanie.

- Asher's Box. This granite memorial box
  which is still being made, will sit above
  ground like a gravestone would have
  if we had buried Asher. We will fill it
  with sentimental things that would have
  been buried with him. The box will be
  engraved with his name and birthdate
  and perhaps something else.

Shelby called us a few days ago to let us know that she recorded "Too Wonderful (Asher's Song)" in Nashville. The producer who she's been working with added some gorgeous instrumental parts—guitar, mandolin, steel guitar, violin. They're not sure which parts are going to be included in the final product, but they are taking Betsy's and my opinions into consideration. They are also talking with a publisher about getting it ready to play on the radio. Things are turning out well for Shelby and "Asher's Song"!

Betsy has been struggling lately with having a lack of direction. She is goal oriented and her primary goal for the last eight months—the goal of being a mother and having a son to care for—has been taken from her. At first, it wasn't a potent feeling—the loss of a goal. But now that over a month had passed, her lack of direction has taken hold. More than that, we are both at a place where we want to get up and do things, but we also so badly want to do nothing. This oxymoron in our lives has led to boredom. We sometimes sit doing nothing because anything we can think of to do doesn't sound appealing. I don't want to go to work anymore (only two more weeks until summer break, at least) and Betsy feels lost because she doesn't have anything she's working toward.

To help remedy this, Betsy and I have spent some time discussing activities that she could pursue either for profit or for fun. She's not looking forward to needing to find a job again, so our hope was to find something that she could do for fun that would turn a profit. She bounced around ideas like selling home-made dog treats, starting a podcast, and volunteering to do some digital marketing for the animal shelter where we found Leo. We spent the most time yesterday playing with the idea of doing a podcast. She has come up with a great idea—all it's going to take now is the drive to make it happen. I really hope she finds something soon. Maybe going back to massage therapy school will help.

Later in the evening, we had some friends over to celebrate Asher's life and enjoy each other's company.

It was great to have some time with close friends who we haven't seen much in the last month. We had a few drinks and talked of normal, happy things—mutual friends we haven't seen in a long time, old teachers, dogs and cats, funny stories. We toasted Asher and shared his pictures and story. Every time we share his story I feel a little better, especially when we get to share it with people who are special to us.

May 18, 2016

L ast night was a beautiful yet sad night. We attended our first support group for parents who have lost babies—a club that nobody wants to join. The people we met were amazing. I am beyond happy with how the evening progressed.

We went back to Parkview for the first time since we left a month and a half ago. After dinner in the cafeteria, we went to the chaplaincy's conference room where the Healing Hearts support group was held. Some people were already there when we came in. We saw Cori, our patient care technician from the hospital, and it was so great to see her again. She probably won't ever know how important she is—she may understand that she's important, but she will never know to what extent she changed my life.

Cori and Kristen led the group together. Both women have experienced the loss of a child and are ideal people to run such a group. There were four other mothers there that night (no other fathers besides myself). The conversation started light—talk of normal things and not about the hurt that each of us shared. When the conversation lulled and introductions were over, the topic of Mother's Day was brought up, and people shared how the day went for them. This topic led to other discussions, some relatable, others not.

Through the conversations, I came to one great realization: Betsy and I are so blessed to have each other and our support system. Some of these other mothers have spouses who didn't want to talk about the child they lost. This is beyond my comprehension and breaks my heart. I can't imagine not being able to talk about Asher, let alone not *wanting* to talk about him. Betsy and I have great family and friends who we can count on as well. We are great communicators and the more we communicate, the better we feel. One topic of conversation was working through the grief. One cannot simply "get over" the grief; it must be faced head-on. It must be experienced. Without that, the healing cannot happen. We have experienced our grief and are continuing to experience it. In a way, it makes Asher more real, more alive, and more present.

Near the end of the session, we shared Shelby's song with everyone there. Tears were shed by all. This was the only group of people who I *knew* would be able to relate to everything the song had to offer. It was a special moment and I hope it meant as much to them as it did to me.

Playing the song opened a connection with one of the ladies there. It turned out that she knew Shelby! She grew up with Shelby's boyfriend. She had met her before and follows her on Facebook. This led to other connections as well. She is married to a band director who I know from a class in college. I had actually followed the story of the loss of their son online. I saw when he was born and the short days that followed until his passing. My heart broke for them then and broke again when I realized who she was. The world is a small place, and God has a way of bringing people together.

The session ended, and Betsy and I ended up

staying an extra hour and forty minutes in conversation with Cori and Kristen. We shared more, they shared more, and we grew to understand each other a little more. It was a special time that I am glad we had. Healing Hearts is a great place for us. Now we can share Asher's story with other people who know what our pain is like, and hopefully, we can find a way to give back to everyone too.

The day passed, and early evening came. We told everyone that we weren't going to keep him much longer—we didn't want his body to start to lose its color, for him to not look like our son anymore. This was a hard realization to come to, but it came, and it was the best choice.

My family was the first to leave. Ashton left earlier than the rest; she looked at Asher and gave him her final goodbye. We told my family that they could be with him as long as they wanted—together or alone. Betsy's family left to give them some time. My mom and dad each held him once more while they mourned his passing. Brittney held him too and said that she wanted some time alone with him. We all left, including Betsy and me, and gave Brittney that time with her nephew. I do not know what passed between them, but I hope it gave Brittney the closure that she needed. When she was done, I came back and took him and told them goodbye. They left and would never see our precious baby again.

Betsy's family stayed longer, but their time came too. When they knew they were going to leave soon, they each had their turn to say goodbye. All of them held him and shared something special.

When Emily told him goodbye, she played the song "Glory Bound" by the Wailin' Jennys from her phone. When the song came to the last chorus of "Hallelujah," she sang with them. You could hear the pain in her voice and the effort it took her to sing to him. To help her along, Abby harmonized with as much strength as Emily. It was one of the most beautiful and heart-wrenching things I have ever heard. Later, Kathy gave us a gift: a framed print of the lyrics of the song with a tree in the background, made by a friend. It now sits on our piano next to Asher's urn.

When Kathy had her last moments with her only grandchild, she played the song "Bright Morning Stars Are Rising" by Abigail Washburn. The song was peaceful, and that's what she wanted for Asher—

peace.

They left soon after, and Betsy and I were once again left alone with our son.

May 24, 2016

It's the last week of school! I am really looking forward to spending the summer with Betsy. This may be the last summer when we both will be off work and able to spend all our time together. Next year she may be working, and I may be working with the high school marching band, so this time together now is precious. I anticipate spending a lot of time working on our house and making our garden a beautiful tribute to Asher. We've already gotten started (with the gracious help of Aunt Wendy and Emily), and things are starting to come together.

On Saturday, my mom and I went to an antique

toy show in Kalamazoo. We went last year for the first time with my dad. This year he had to work, so it was just my mom and me. I was supposed to have a community band concert, but I decided that I'm not quite ready to go back. The only rehearsal I went to after we lost Asher was just "off." I didn't want to be there. The main reason I went was so I could spend a little time with Adam. Taking a break is what's best for me now. I'm sure that one day (probably this summer) I will want to go back—just not yet.

Anyway, my mom and I road-tripped to Kalamazoo for this toy show. The majority of the conversation was focused on Asher. We talked about so many things: how everyone was doing, how my mom (and Betsy and I) think that Leo was a godsend for us, how different people were still holding Asher's memory close, how plans were going for his memorial. This time talking about my baby was special. I think it was the first long one-on-one conversation I've had with my mother (or anyone besides Betsy) about him. The more I talk about him, the more I am aware of how much I love him. I know that I love him with all my heart but talking about it makes the love more present.

The show itself was a lot of fun and a great way

for my mom and me to bond. While I didn't find anything to buy for myself, the whole trip was worth it.

Emily was visiting this weekend. It was great to
have her around, especially because Betsy got to spend
time with her. Besides gardening, their big weekend
project was to find a way to waterproof some colored
mandalas, which will hang in Asher's section of the
garden. Betsy has been coloring mandalas for Asher
as a coping mechanism. She encouraged Emily to join
her. After trial and error, I think they finally found a
way to cover the mandalas (copies of them, just in
case it didn't work out) in resin so they can hang outside in the weather. While it isn't cheap to buy the
resin, the result is wonderful. I think that after a while
(and maybe a little bit of saving to buy enough resin),
the garden will have a wonderfully colorful area filled
with mandalas.

Today is my mom's 51st birthday. I really hope
it's a good one for her. I think we will have time this
evening to go visit for a while. We went out to eat at
Bill's Steakhouse in Bronson, MI, on Sunday. Emily
got to join us as well. Besides the good feelings of
good food and spending time with the family, lunch
was also kind of sad. Paisley was there with Ashton
and Ryne and it was, as it has been, saddening to see

the baby who was supposed to be Asher's childhood friend and playmate. The hardest thing, though, is forcing myself to be happy to see her. It isn't hard to be happy, but it is hard not to lament what will never be. She is my one and only niece (for now) and I want to love her and be with her because we will not get these moments back. I need to spend time with her, although it may be hard for now.

***

This next stage was one of the most meaningful and sorrowful parts of my life. We knew that we could keep Asher as long as we wanted, but we also knew that this was the time. The time to say goodbye. There was nothing else to do with his physical presence. We had gotten pictures and spent time with him. Prolonging the inevitable would just be harder. It was time.

I took my son in my arms and went to sit on the couch. Betsy joined me. I passed him to his mother. For a long while, we just sat with him. We looked at him. We loved him. This was our last time together as a family and we knew it.

Betsy gave him back to me, so I could have one more special moment with my baby. At this point, I did the second hardest thing I have ever done. I read to him a book that I hoped to read to him later—*Love You Forever*. I could barely make it through, but I knew I had to. I sobbed and read quietly. I will never be able to read this book with any of my future children. It has a special place in my heart that is filled with the memory of Asher.

I talked with him afterward. I told him how much I love him and how much he means to both Betsy and me. I told him to be with his mommy in the night to bring her comfort and rest.

I gave Asher to Betsy, so she could have one more special moment with her baby. She talked to him then too. She told him how much she loves him and how much he means to both of us. She talked about her thoughts, hopes, and dreams for him and all the things she will never be able to share with him. She told him to come to me in my dreams and to let us know that everything is all right.

Betsy stood and brought him over to the bed. She undressed him, so he was just as God intended him to look. She bent over him and kissed him. She kissed him everywhere as she cried. She baptized him in her tears. This moment was special to see, but it was not for me—it was for Betsy and Asher. This moment meant more to her than most anything in her life.

Afterward, she held Asher and we hugged. A long, meaningful hug, knowing that our family would never be together like this again.

Betsy then gave Asher the gift of music. She gave him the song "You Are My Sunshine." This was Betsy's song that her mother sang to her. It was my song that my mother sang to me. It is now more prominently Asher's song. Like my story, we will never be able to share it with any of our future children.

Betsy lay down in bed for one last skin-to-skin time with Asher. I lay beside her and we just existed for a while. We existed and loved. We were together. We were as whole as we could be. We just—were. Time passed.

Betsy felt moved to sing again. She sang the song "Misty." It was beautiful and perfect. Because I knew that I would never get another chance, I sang too. I sang "Lullaby" from the musical *The Scarlet Pimpernel*. It was all that I could think of at the time, and I needed to share something. A lullaby seemed appropriate. We lay even longer, just being.

Betsy wanted me to have some skin-to-skin time with him too. I would have wanted this had he been living, but it wasn't something I wanted then. He was cold. So, so cold. When I looked at my baby, I could almost pretend he was asleep. His eyes were closed. I couldn't see him breathing, but you can't always see that when they're all wrapped up. He wasn't moving, but babies don't always move when they sleep. When I touched him, though, he was cold. Babies are not supposed to be cold. They are warm. Always warm. This was a struggle I had ever since I first touched him. He was always too cold to be alive. I didn't want to remember that feeling. Having skin-to-skin time would burn that feeling into my skin. After some convincing though, I did. I knew that I could never have another opportunity. I took off my shirt and Betsy and I both had that time together with Asher. As I thought, the cool of his skin was painful to feel. But I did what I knew I must. As we lay there, Betsy fell asleep. I did not.

Later, Betsy woke up and it was time for me to start moving again. When I got up, Betsy told me to feel him. A miracle had happened. He was warm. I believe with all my heart that God helped our bodies warm his to the point where he felt as he should. I smiled and cried. My baby boy was warm like all babies. I will never forget that feeling and the elation I felt. I still thank God for that moment.

I went out to let the nurses know that we were almost ready to say goodbye. When security came to take him away, we wanted a few more minutes with him to say our final goodbye.

I went back in and we took off his ankle bracelet to keep. We also took a few locks of his hair. We will forever know what it was like. Around this time, I touched Asher like my father touched me. I took my fingers and moved them so gently down his forehead and nose. This movement used to put my siblings and me to sleep—I still do it to myself sometimes. I shared that moment with him for his final and permanent sleep.

One of Betsy's desires was to massage her baby frequently. Touch is an important, personal, and intimate thing that should be shared with a child. She massaged Asher, taking great care. She gave him as much touch as she could in our final minutes with him. Betsy's primary love language is quality time. As time was so short, her second love language took the forefront—touch. I am so happy that she had that time with him.

When security came to take him, we took our last moments with our son and drank them in as much as we could, knowing that we would not have enough of it. We gathered together, and I took out my phone to play "Asher's Theme." Betsy wrote the piano piece for him months before. She played it for him frequently. At his last ultrasound before we lost him, we played it for him to get him to move. This was his song. Written for him and performed by his mother. This is the last thing that we wanted to come from us.

When it was over, they came in. It was then that I did the hardest thing I will probably ever do. I took my baby from his mother, who would never hold her beloved child again. I walked over to where they had placed a basket and placed him inside. Laying him down, I took my last look at my one and only son, and they closed the lid.

They left with the most precious part of our lives. With the basket went a piece of our hearts that we will never get back. I went back into the bed with Betsy, and we mourned.

June 2, 2016

It's been over a week since I journaled last. Something about putting an end to Asher's story in this world seemed to put a sense of finality over me. I no longer felt that I needed to write so often. I think this may be a coming trend. I do not feel that I need to write as a coping mechanism any longer. Instead, my writing will be to remember and to keep a record of my coming thoughts and feelings. I hope other grieving parents can read my words and find some comfort in knowing that others have gone through this stage of life too.

School is now over, and I have (seemingly)

more time on my hands. Alas, this first week off has been quite busy. We've already gotten started on the summer "to-do" list, but mostly we have been preparing our house for guests. This weekend Andy, Kathy, and Abby are staying with us. Saturday will be Asher's funeral.

We met with Pastor Ruth yesterday to talk about how we want the funeral to go. While we weren't really prepared with thoughts and ideas of what we wanted, Ruth had done her research and had a lot of ideas to share with us. Over an hour passed before we finished planning. We are so thankful for all that Ruth has done for us in planning his memorial. She has tenderly and lovingly helped us prepare a special ceremony for our baby.

Following the funeral, which will only be for immediate family and Asher's great-grandparents, we will go out for lunch, then hold an open house at my parents' home. We decided a while ago that, instead of having a full funeral for anyone to attend, we would have a party in Asher's memory. We especially wanted to have people there to share in music making. Some of Betsy's and my most tangible and moving memories involve making music with others. Asher would have been a part of that. We want him to be a part of it now.

I started reading a book about grieving fathers called *Strong and Tender*. My mom got it for me a while ago, and I'm just now getting around to reading it. Many parts of it aren't necessarily relevant to me, but I can see how they would be impactful for others. Other parts, though, are exactly what I need at this point. I especially enjoy the quotes and poems throughout.

One quote from Steve Richter describes how he perceives the difference between a man's and woman's feelings about losing a child. He feels that a woman tends to feel as if something was taken from her, while a man feels as if something was never given to him. I agree with this on many points—especially the word "tends." I appreciate that Mr. Richter didn't assume that all people feel the same. As far as I'm concerned, I would say I 80% feel that something was never given to me and 20% feel that something has been taken from me. While I did not carry Asher in my womb and feel him as a part of my body, I did feel him. I talked to him, I felt him kick, I looked at his face in the ultrasounds. I knew him as much as any father could. I knew that he would move when I read to him. I knew that he liked to dance across my hand when I felt Betsy's tummy. I knew that he knew I was his father. Those feelings were taken away. Even though he never took a single breath of air on this Earth, I know that we knew each other.

June 15, 2016

I know it's been two weeks since I last wrote in this journal, but like I said in my last entry, I no longer desperately need to use writing as a coping mechanism. I thought I would need to write after the funeral—I did not. I thought I would need to write after his memorial party—I did not. I thought I would need to write after we released a lantern for deceased children—I did not. I thought I would need to write at *some point* in the last two weeks—I did not.

I am writing now, not because I have the need to, but because I want to. I am (almost) beyond the part of this journal that is for my own needs. Now, I hope to journal for those people who will read this. I write so they may find comfort in seeing my story continue beyond the tragedy. I want to express what I can and hope that it brings some comfort and acceptance for what is.

For my own benefit, so I can forever remember:

Asher's funeral was perfect. Pastor Ruth spoke with such care, and her message was exactly right for Asher. Those who wanted to speak, spoke. Betsy played Asher's theme, and I cried harder than anyone else. We sang hymns. The service was short like Asher's life.

After the service and lunch, we went back to my parent's house for the party, and we were *shocked* by the turnout. Unfortunately, it rained a little, so everyone was inside. At times there were over fifty people there at one time. It was wonderful to see so many people come out to show us support and to show their love for Asher. We had people color mandalas in lieu of gifts, and we received so many. I was so happy we decided to have this memorial. I would have changed nothing.

Just a few days ago, we got together with our support group and released lanterns into the sky. Family and friends were invited as well. We wrote messages to our children on the lanterns before we let them fly into the night sky. I look forward to doing this again next year.

In hopes of bringing comfort:

My life is different. I will never again be the person I was before I received the phone call from Betsy with the news of my child's death. But this is all okay. Yes, I have only been a childless father for two months and four days. Yes, this may seem like too short of a timespan to start being "okay" with my new life. But all my feelings are "okay." It is okay for me to feel however I need to feel.

I am blessed in *so* many ways. One of the biggest blessings so far has been my acceptance. I have accepted the empty place in my heart that will always belong to Asher. I have accepted that I will not get to raise my first-born child. I have accepted that I will never be able to hold my son again in this lifetime. I have accepted that Betsy and I will have to wait to have more children. I have accepted that Asher's too-short life has been a blessing to many people. I have accepted my feelings. I have accepted that I love someone so much, even though I barely know him. I have accepted that my life is different.

NOT EVERYONE WILL FEEL THIS WAY.

I put this in all caps to enunciate how strongly I feel this statement. I do not think it is common to feel as I do after only two months.

To all grieving mothers and fathers who read this: know that how you are feeling now is *okay*. As long as you are safe and supporting your partner or whoever else is grieving with you, you can feel however you need to at this time and for all future times. Do not feel guilty if you are feeling like you're on the mend or even completely finished with your grieving. You are *not* doing any disservice to your lost child by not thinking about them constantly.

If you need to grieve openly, grieve openly. If you need to talk with your partner, talk with your partner. If you need to celebrate your child's life, celebrate your child's life. If you need to laugh and cry at the same time, laugh and cry at the same time. If you need to seclude yourself from the world for a day or two, seclude yourself from the world for a day or two. *Do what you need to do.* Period. No grieving looks the same. There is no set time period for your grief. Be you through this whole process and do what is best for you.

Men, do not feel that you must always be strong. Sometimes strength is necessary, but that goes for anyone. Have no shame when weakness comes. Embrace it. Cry. Weep. Sob. Share. Talk. Laugh. Hug. Love. There is no weakness in grieving the loss of a child. Accept your feelings and embrace them. *All* of them.

As I said before, I have been so fortunate to have such supportive family and friends to help me with my grieving. This has worked for me. Betsy and I are great communicators who talk through all our feelings, and the conversations bring us to acceptance. If you feel that you have no one to talk to, find someone. Join a community online of other people who have been through this. Go see a grief counselor. Find a support group in your area. Make a new friend or call a family member you haven't seen in a long time. Call me! You need to communicate your feelings—otherwise, they will fester and become a problem rather than a solution.

Understanding may not come, but acceptance can if you let it.

June 20, 2016

Yesterday was my first Father's Day. While parts were hard—thinking of what could have been, for example—most of the day was good. Betsy and I spent it as a couple and did some nice things together to celebrate. We each had our own day to spend with our own fathers, but today was a day for us. We did some reminiscing and planting in Asher's Garden in our courtyard. We also relaxed together, went out for lunch, and went to the drive-in movie theater in the evening. It was a nice day, but I wish we could have had our son with us.

I had a ring with Asher's name inscribed on the

outside made for Father's Day. It's gorgeous and perfect. I love that he is always close to me in this way. Also, Betsy surprised me with a gift that means even more—*Love You Forever* in a frame. But this wasn't just a copy of the book, it was *the* book. The exact one that I read to Asher before we said goodbye. Betsy went to the hospital and asked for the book to give to me. I am overwhelmed with how much this gift means to me. We will be purchasing another copy, and other books too, to donate to the hospital in Asher's name.

I want to take a moment to share some thoughts with all men reading this who have lost their baby and have no other children:

You are a father. Never let anyone tell you differently. You love your child just as much as any other man loves his son or daughter. Even though you no longer have your child in your arms, you are still a father.

Take your Father's Day and experience it however you feel you need to. If you need to be secluded in your home for the day, do so. If you want to share your child's story with a friend you haven't seen in a while, do so. If you want to celebrate your child's life with your partner, do so. If you want to try to have a day with no tears, do so. Whatever you need, do what you need to do. You are a father.

June 30, 2016

When we first found out that we were going to have a baby, we weren't going to share the baby's name with anyone. I didn't want to hear anybody's opinion because the only opinions that mattered were Betsy's and mine. But, because Betsy and I are who we are, we got so excited about Asher's name that we just needed to share it with someone.

I am so thankful that the circumstances led us to sharing the name with our immediate family. We still didn't share his name with the world via social media or any other means because we wanted there to be some element of surprise and people tend to be crueler on social media when hearing names they don't like. So, we ended up telling my parents, Betsy's parents, all our siblings, and a few close friends.

The reason that I'm thankful is that people were comfortable using Asher's name before he was even here. When the time came that we lost him, it was as if he was already a part of the family and not someone who had just entered it. This is a gift (albeit an accidental one) that I wouldn't trade for anything. Asher was a part of our lives before he was born, and he continues to be a part of our lives today. Using his name earlier than he was actually with us made him feel more present.

When we conceive our next child, I want to share his or her name with our family again. God forbid we should lose another child, but I don't want to risk our next child not being a part of our family in name even before he or she is born. I will ensure that we give ourselves that gift again.

July 10, 2016

A few days ago, we purchased a George Peebles painting of a tree. As we expected (and we would have accepted nothing less), it is perfect.

On July 5 (our second wedding anniversary), we decided to take a trip to Elkhart, IN, to look at more paintings by George Peebles. After trying to contact the initial gallery we went to in Traverse City about a commission and not hearing back, we thought it would be a good idea to see if Asher's painting had already been created. The gallery in Elkhart had a few paintings, but not many. The gallery owner graciously let us borrow the one painting that we thought we liked to see how it looked in our space. After a nice lunch and some other shopping in Elkhart, we took the piece home.

The painting went up, and we knew. This wasn't the one. I wanted to live with it for a few days to see if it grew on me, but deep down, I knew it wouldn't.

The next day, Betsy suggested returning the painting to Elkhart and visiting a couple more galleries up in Michigan. Since we didn't have anything going on that day, I agreed and (after getting a dog sitter) we left.

We first drove the hour and a half to Elkhart to return the first painting. That was followed by another hour and a half drive to Holland, MI. The gallery there had *many* pieces by Mr. Peebles, so we were hopeful that we would find the one. We looked and looked. Two paintings were *almost* what we wanted. We eventually narrowed it down to one (the other painting had a couple of weird strokes that looked like the face of Voldemort from Harry Potter—that couldn't be unseen). Our decision was to go look in a final gallery in Grand Rapids (only half an hour away), and if we didn't find one that we loved more, we would come back or decide to commission a work through another gallery.

The drive to Grand Rapids was short (thank goodness). We went into this final gallery—Mercury Head Gallery—and immediately saw the Peebles paintings lined up, ready to peruse.

The space from the top of our fireplace to the ceiling was exactly 48 inches. Because of this, I didn't want to look at any piece that was too big—I didn't want to fall in love with something that I couldn't have. The smaller pieces were beautiful, but not what we were looking for. Betsy decided to look at the big ones anyway and pulled one out.

It was everything we could have imagined. The tree's leaves were made of vibrant reds, oranges, yellows, greens, purples, teals, and blues. The ground was striking purple and dry yellow. The sky stretched up a cold blue with wispy clouds. A small pond was visible through the violet underbrush. The tree stood tall and otherworldly. The season was not spring, summer, fall, or winter—it was all of them and none of them. Forever frozen in time in a beauty that cannot be found on this Earth. In it, we saw Asher.

But it was too big. I shut down and wanted to put it away. Betsy (in her stubborn way that I love) wasn't giving up so easily. "We can't have it," I said.

"But it's everything we want," she said. Back and forth discussing options.

The owner then got involved in the conversation. She told us that it would be possible to restretch the canvas to a smaller size, but some of the sky at the top would need to be taken off. The sky was the least important part of the painting, and we could do without. We had told her the story of Asher, and she wanted to make sure we had the perfect piece. While Mr. Peebles could try to recreate the painting via a commission, she said, it probably wouldn't come back exactly the same. We wanted exactly the same. We needed exactly the same.

The problem was that buying and resizing the piece cost more than to commission a new piece. After much debate, we decided to pay the amount of the full size plus the restretching fee to ensure that we had the ideal piece. This was a wonderful decision.

We shopped and visited a microbrewery while the painting was being restretched, talking about how excited we were all the while. We returned after an hour or so, and it was ready. Absolutely flawless.

When we went to settle the bill, we found that (presumably because of Asher), they had charged us for a smaller painting. This saved us over $300. I am still blown away every time people do generous and kind things for us. Asher has truly touched the lives of so many and has led them to good deeds and goodwill. I am an advocate for "paying it forward," but I don't know if I can ever pay enough forward to make up for all the generosity and kindness that has been shown to us. I am humbled.

The painting now hangs over our fireplace, and it is just as Asher always will be—perfect.

July 12, 2016

I miss Asher today. So much.

I'm in Elkhart now, just finishing a professional development day. The professional development itself was really great—I learned a lot and had a lot of fun. But this morning, after I woke up and got ready, I was very sad on the drive to the PD. I haven't really felt this amount of sadness in a while, and it's unfortunate that it had to happen on a day that I needed to be at my professional best.

Throughout the day, I found myself not paying attention to what was going on and just thinking about him. The time he was still alive within Betsy, the brief time we had him here, and the future he would never have.

At dinner this evening, I found myself trying to bring him up in a conversation. In most circumstances, I don't have any problem talking about him, and I wouldn't have had any trouble talking about him this evening. But, alas, I was around people who I don't really know. They didn't know that I had recently lost a child. And why should I bring that up over a nice dinner and conversation? I found myself trying to direct conversations toward children in the hopes that someone would ask me if I had any, to which I would respond, "Yes, I have a son in heaven."

The question didn't come. I wish it had.

July 28, 2016

We made a mistake by going on a family vacation with my almost ten-month-old niece. Going to Florida to relax at the beach sounded really nice. We thought we could handle being around the baby for long periods of time. We were wrong.

This has been the hardest week for Betsy since the weeks immediately following our loss. Tears have been shed every day for various reasons. Thinking of what Asher won't have, seeing Asher's grandparents happy with another grandchild, watching other parents get to *be* parents, seeing baby items everywhere in the condo, thinking of how our lives were supposed to be. These things have been hard on us both, but harder on Betsy.

For better or worse, I am well-versed in pushing bad feelings out of the forefront of my mind so that I can find the best in situations. This has helped me out a lot this week. While I don't always do that (in fact, I fully experience my emotions when I can), I have done it this week, which put Betsy and me in two different places. Not being in the same emotional place makes it harder for us to communicate and agree on some things. This has been a challenge this week as well.

On top of the mountain of grief, a minor inconvenience or "feather-ruffling" becomes a much bigger problem. Little things, such as cleaning up the space for someone else when they were supposed to, become large problems. Being chastised for being too loud when others are trying to sleep brings on anger and resentment much faster than it would if we weren't also trying our best to ignore all our feelings of loss. Regular family squabbling isn't easy to look past because it feels like we are being doubly punished for having a dead child. Not only do we have to see baby things everywhere, but we also have to be a part of petty grievances, which are now a big deal.

Nothing about this week is fair. Nothing in life is fair. It's not fair that we need to be bothered about being too loud. It's not fair that we need to clean up other people's messes. It's not fair that we need to look at baby things everywhere. It's not fair that we don't have our son with us.

All of this aside, I want peace. I want the last couple days of this vacation to go smoothly, without tears. I want to talk with everyone who we have had an issue with or who has had an issue with us so that we can forgive and forget. Unfortunately for my parents, there have been issues in the past with their siblings and in-laws that have led to relationships not being as tight as they should be. Problems would arise, and no one would talk about them. Grudges were held, and no resolution came. My parents cannot go on family vacations with some of their siblings because of rocky relationships—something they regret.

I need to have a good relationship with all my siblings and in-laws. I will bring up disputes until they are resolved if need be. I have a low negativity threshold, and I refuse to keep negativity in my family. I love and respect them too much for that.

August 5, 2016

Life has been pretty crazy since we got back from vacation. Our last few days were much better. We discussed some problems, clearing the air. I like to think of the last couple days as our real vacation. Snorkeling was a lot of fun, and it turned out to be a pretty impactful experience for both Betsy and me. It's definitely good to be home, though.

The night we got back, Betsy had trouble sleeping. As she does sometimes, she decided to get on Petfinder for fun to see which dogs are looking for homes. Unfortunately/fortunately, she found a dog who needed *our* home. His name was Louie, and he was an even-tempered mini dachshund like Leo.

We didn't *need* another dog, but we thought Leo would like to have company when both Betsy and I go back to work. We decided to go meet him at an adopt-a-thon happening in Ohio. When we got there, he wasn't there—he was at his foster's home. We got in contact with his foster and made plans to meet Louie the next day.

When we got together to meet Louie, we knew that we would be getting another dog. He and Leo got along well. They were about the same size, and they acted similarly—both very laid-back. It was "love at first smell" for them.

We've had him home for five days now, and things have been going well! But with a new dog, going back to work, and still dealing with the challenges of grief, life has been pretty chaotic. Hopefully, it calms down soon.

August 26, 2016

It's been a while since I've written. Life has started to get back into a "normal" flow and time has gotten away from me.

Quick update on life—I love teaching at the middle school. I am so happy to be teaching band after many years of anticipating this type of job. Betsy started substitute teaching in my school corporation as well, so she can start bringing in some money and we can carpool sometimes.

We are working on redoing the stairs in our house and making other small updates to help make the house feel more like home. We received Asher's memorial box for our garden—it's beautiful.

Leo and Louie are still getting along well, even though Leo constantly shows his dominance. Hopefully, they'll be completely house-trained soon.

Lately, life's been a little more difficult, especially for Betsy. It's been about four-and-a-half months since we lost Asher, and it's starting to feel like other people in our lives are moving on. We know that this sentiment is only half true. We are still grieving heavily, while others have more easily fallen back into their normal routines. Not everyone is thinking about Asher as much as when his loss was fresh. However, part of this feeling comes from the fact that people don't talk about Asher as much anymore. Betsy and I talk about him, of course, but everyone else talks about him much less.

This, however, does *not* mean that they've moved on. After bringing up briefly this sentiment on social media, we heard from so many people (family and friends alike) who still think about Asher every day. For some, Betsy and I are still constantly in their prayers. Some people have even let us know that they don't think they will ever stop thinking about him.

This is definitely true for family. Our family still tells us about times when their lives seem to stop as they are reminded of Asher. I need to remind myself often that our families have been deeply affected by his loss too, and they won't move on any more than we will. "Moving on" will never be a thing for any of us. "Acceptance" is what we anticipate.

Betsy and I both took the day off today as a "mental recuperation" day. Life is overwhelming right now. Grieving, working again, making improvements to the house, cleaning, needing more money, spending too much money, and a plethora of other obligations have been too much of late. We needed this day of rest and relaxation to feel whole again.

We've decided to investigate grief therapy for the near future. I think I am closer to the "acceptance" part of my journey than Betsy is. Lately, because of life's stresses, Betsy has been so overwhelmed with everything that she's been at the lowest point I've ever seen her. It pains me to see her in a downward spiral of despair. If one thing isn't good, it leads to another, and so on until it's almost too hard to handle. I believe a lot of this has to do with where she is in the grieving process. I pray that grief therapy will teach us how to cope a little better.

In those times of deepest despair, there is little I can do to help. Sometimes, I can calm the situation just by being present, talking about happier things, or letting her express her feelings to me. Other times, I can't help at all. I don't like feeling helpless. As her husband, I feel that I need to be her constant and her rock. I express my feelings to her because I know that it's important for me to share too. But sometimes, I feel like I'm not doing enough to help her because I am at a loss for what to do. Hopefully, grief therapy will help us learn what works during those times.

I love Betsy too much for anything bad to happen to her. She is the best thing that has ever happened to me. Life would be almost unbearable without her. She feels the same way about me.

To all the fathers of baby angels: be there for your partner. She needs you so badly, and you need her. There is no one else in this world who knows exactly what you're going through. Others who have lost children can empathize. The child's grandparents and families can grieve. Friends can grieve for you, and anyone can sympathize, but not one single person besides you and your partner knows what it is like to lose YOUR child. Be there for her and she will be there for you.

Life suggestions for now and forever:

To Support Your Partner:

- Talk to her about your baby.
- Tell her your feelings regularly.
- Listen to her thoughts and feelings.
- Ask her hard questions like, "How are you feeling about [baby's name] today?" or "Have you thought about hurting yourself in the hopes of seeing [baby's name] soon?" or "Do you think you are falling into depression?" Her answers may not be what you expect, or they might open the door into a serious discussion. This may be the only way to know whether your partner needs professional help (especially the questions about self-harm). Some questions can and should be asked daily.
- Love your spouse (and other children if you have them) more than you've ever loved her before.

To Remember:

- Honor your baby in your house with pictures or anything to remember him or her visually.
- Take time to think deeply about your child.
- Bring up your child whenever you want to. Don't worry about whether it makes other people uncomfortable—you're bringing it up because it's what *you* need.
- Look at the pictures of your child if you have any. If you don't have any, look at ultrasound pictures; if you don't have any of those, look at anything that reminds you of your baby.

To Support Yourself:

- Ask yourself the same questions about reflection or self-harm that you asked your spouse.
- Ask others for help when you need it— you're not made of stone, and you're not Superman.
- Cry whenever you feel like it.
- Be aware of your needs, and make sure they're being accounted for.
- Love your whole family more deeply.
- Count your blessings. I mean this in a literal sense—remind yourself of the good things in your life. I guarantee you have more than you think.

September 1, 2016

I am sad.

I am sad because of grief. I am sad because of shaky family relationships. I am sad because of a lack of money. I am sad because of a crappy week at work. I am sad because I feel unhealthy. I am sad because of life right now.

This will change.

This will change because money will come. This will change because relationships endure and move past hardships. This will change because work has its ups and downs (mostly ups). This will change because I can alter my lifestyle to help me feel healthier. This will change because I have control over my emotions and how I perceive the world. This will change because time will lead to acceptance of our loss.

I will be happy once again.

September 3, 2016

Last night, Betsy and I watched *Inside Out*. While I had seen the movie before, it took on a different meaning since we lost Asher.

For being a kid's movie, *Inside Out* has some deep themes and is an interesting way to view our thoughts and emotions. The primary takeaway from the movie is that memories can change, and they can be both happy and sad. When we accept that we can have multiple emotions simultaneously, we can better accept the world around us. Being "happy-sad" (feeling both emotions at once) is a challenging way to be. It's hard to accept that we can be both at the same time.

Losing Asher has been a sad time for all of us affected by his loss. However, our grief has not stopped us from noticing the good things that peek out and shine their light down upon us.

I count my blessings every day. These blessings include sentiments that are hard to think about. Here are some things that I feel "happy-sad" about:

- I never heard my baby cry. I lament that I will never know what he sounded like, but his cries will not haunt my dreams forever.
- My baby had a quick and painless death. He died, but in the easiest way possible.
- His entire life was surrounded by warmth and love. He wanted for nothing and never knew the woes of the outside world. But, he never knew the outside world.
- My wife got to carry my son. Betsy experienced his entire life inside her, which is a wonderful thing. It is saddening to know that I will never know him like she did.

- My baby moved when he heard my voice. I would read and sing to Asher while he was in the womb, and he would move whenever I did so. I never got to experience that while holding him.

- Asher made Betsy and me better parents. Our future children will be loved and appreciated even more because we know what it's like to not be able to share our love with our child anymore.

- Our family bonds are stronger. Both sides of our families are more closely bonded because we grieve together. Asher will never see the change in us on this Earth.

- Betsy and I have been through the hardest thing we will (hopefully) ever go through. We now have a better idea of how we will respond to future tragedies and deaths.

Here are some things that I hope to be "happy-sad" about one day:

- I want to remember holding Asher and smile at the thought of holding my firstborn child.
- I want to look at the memorials for Asher in our garden and fully appreciate how beautiful and meaningful they are.
- I want to hear "Asher's Theme" and feel joy.
- I want to share Asher's story with my future children and feel content that they will know their older brother as well as any of us.

September 18, 2016

L ife is hard. In this particular moment, life is weighing down on me. I am plagued with stress over money (or lack thereof), stress from work, stress over housework/cleaning, stress over housetraining dogs, stress from needing to be healthier. All these things affect people in their mid-twenties and beyond.

But my underlying stress is less typical of those my age. I am grieving daily for my son. I am concerned about our next pregnancy. I'm concerned about when we can even start trying to get pregnant (we are going to Costa Rica for Abby and Rodrigo's wedding in November, and the Zika virus is still down there). I am concerned about financially supporting a child when he or she arrives. I am concerned that Betsy won't find the help she needs from a grief counselor (she has an introductory session tomorrow). I am concerned for Betsy's happiness, health, and well-being.

There are points when I don't know what to do. For most of my life, I have had the "it will turn out okay in the end" mentality. I am still like this most of the time, but sometimes everything is just so overwhelming that it's hard to find that positive outlook.

I need to count my blessings. There are plenty. Hopefully, this will help me relax so I can go to sleep.

September 29, 2016

Brittney shared an article on Facebook with me today about grief. It originally came from a Reddit user called GSnow. I would like to share it now, so I can always remember the analogy that I think accurately describes my grief:

Someone on Reddit wrote the following heartfelt plea online:

"My friend just died. I don't know what to do."

A lot of people responded. Then there's one old guy's incredible comment that stood out from the rest that might just change the way we approach life and death:

"Alright, here goes. I'm old. What that means is that I've survived (so far), and a lot of people I've known and loved did not. I've lost friends, best friends, acquaintances, co-workers, grandparents, mom, relatives, teachers, mentors, students, neighbors, and a host of other folks. I have no children, and I can't imagine the pain it must be to lose a child. But here's my two cents.

"I wish I could say you get used to people dying. I never did. I don't want to. It tears a hole through me whenever somebody I love dies, no matter the circumstances. But I don't want it to "not matter." I don't want it to be something that just passes. My scars are a testament to the love and the relationship that I had for and with that person. And if the scar is deep, so was the love. So be it. Scars are a testament to life. Scars are a testament that I can love deeply and live deeply and be cut, or even gouged, and that I can heal and continue to live and continue to love. And the scar tissue is stronger than the original flesh ever was. Scars are a testament to life. Scars are only ugly to people who can't see.

"As for grief, you'll find it comes in waves. When the ship is first wrecked, you're drowning, with the wreckage all around you. Everything floating around you reminds you of the beauty and the magnificence of the ship that was and is no more. And all you can do is float. You find some piece of wreckage, and you hang on for a while. Maybe it's some physical thing. Maybe it's a happy memory or a photograph. Maybe it's a person who is also floating. For a while, all you can do it float. Stay alive.

"In the beginning, the waves are 100 feet tall and crash over you without mercy. They come 10 seconds apart and don't even give you time to catch your breath. All you can do is hang on and float. After a while, maybe weeks, maybe months, you'll find the waves are still 100 feet tall, but they come further apart. When they come, they still crash all over you and wipe you out. But in between, you can breathe; you can function. You never know what's going to trigger the grief. It might be a song, a picture, a street intersection, the smell of a cup of coffee. It can be just about anything…and the wave comes crashing. But in between waves, there is life.

"Somewhere down the line, and it's different for everybody, you find that the waves are only 80 feet tall. Or 50 feet tall. And while they still come, they come further apart. You can see them coming. An anniversary, a birthday, or Christmas, or landing at O'Hare. You can see it coming for the most part and prepare yourself. And when it washes over you, you know that somehow you will, again, come out the other side. Soaking wet, sputtering, still hanging on to some tiny piece of the wreckage, but you'll come out.

"Take it from an old guy. The waves never stop coming, and somehow you don't really want them to. But you learn that you'll survive them. And other waves will come. And you'll survive them too. If you're lucky, you'll have lots of scars from lots of loves. And lots of shipwrecks."

October 24, 2016

I haven't been writing for a while. I wish I would have taken the time earlier, so I could have guaranteed that I would remember everything. But life has been busy, so I can't say I'm surprised it's taken me so long.

First of all, "Too Wonderful (Asher's Song)" is out! It's been a pretty great success so far! Shelby released the song on iTunes and Spotify along with an accompanying lyric video on October 7. The video included a lot of Asher's real pictures. It really spoke to a lot of people. Within the first few hours, it had thousands of views, and it currently has over 19,000!

We were extremely happy with the initial turnout. Shelby was even contacted by Pregistry on Facebook to do an interview for their blog. This was a really neat experience, and Shelby hit the nail on the head with Asher's story. She also discussed the breaking of the stigma and taboo of talking about miscarriage and stillbirth. What a great blog post!

October is National Pregnancy and Infant Loss Awareness Month. Betsy and I have been vocal about this on social media to help spread awareness about this too-common occurrence. On October 15, we participated in a walk for pregnancy and infant loss. We proudly and sadly wore stickers with "I walk to remember Asher" written on them. My mom and Paisley joined Betsy and me as we walked through a park with almost 400 other people that day. At the end of the walk, we released balloons for our children. There were too many balloons in the sky that day. We also asked for "Asher's Song" to be played, and they allowed it. I'm not sure how many people were paying attention at the time, but I know those members of our support group heard the song and knew its significance.

We also got the opportunity to be interviewed for a short video for Cuddle Cots. A Cuddle Cot was the piece of equipment that kept Asher's body cool, so we could be with him for a longer period of time. The video included our interview, along with interviews with Cori and some other Parkview Hospital staff members. It turned out well, and I hope that it will be circulated to the point that every hospital has this necessary piece of medical equipment. It changed our experience at the hospital because it allowed us to keep our baby longer.

This seems like a short entry for not having written for almost a month. But there is nothing more to say at this point. Life is moving on. And Betsy and I are finally starting to move with it.

October 26, 2016

I started reading *Vessels: A Love Story* by Daniel Raeburn today. I bought it in the hopes of finding some more literature about losing a child from the perspective of the father. I am hoping that I can relate in some way.

So far, I can relate little. Raeburn had an unfortunate childhood that was unlike mine. But beyond that, he did not *want* his first child. I did. Very much.

His wife's first pregnancy resulted in miscarriage and her second pregnancy ended in stillbirth. I am not far into the book, but from what I have read, the circumstances of the stillbirth were different from ours. They lost their daughter Irene, and Raeburn's wife gave birth naturally rather than with a C-section. Once Irene was born, neither Raeburn nor his wife wanted much to do with her. They had Irene with them for a short amount of time before hospital staff took her away. Raeburn allowed them to do so with no protest.

This story helps me to more fully realize how lucky Betsy and I were to be at Parkview for our loss of Asher. They did everything in their power to ensure that we made the best of our bad experience. I feel bad for Raeburn and his wife for having to go through their loss, but I feel even worse that they did not have an experience like ours that was filled to the brim with support from the hospital, family, and friends.

Perhaps Raeburn would disagree with me, and perhaps the book will shed more light on the situation in the coming pages, but for now, I am sad for him. And I am thankful that my experience was different.

November 2, 2016

Betsy wrote a poem and posted it on Facebook today. I love her and her writing so much. Her words capture thoughts that other mediums cannot. Here's the poem:

Today is a hard day
As I remember
All you were meant to be
To us, your parents
Your family, your friends
Who would all be able to see
Who you'd become

What you'd look like

How you would laugh or you'd smile

But, that's not to be

We won't see those things

For what seems like an awful long while

It's a hard conversation

Most people won't have

About how one's child is dead

But please still remember

My son, oh my Asher,

He's alive,

But is growing wings instead

November 9, 2016

Betsy and I are at the airport now getting ready to leave for Costa Rica for Abby and Rodrigo's wedding. We need a break from life—especially since the election results were just announced a couple of hours ago. I am afraid for the future of our unborn children. I pray that our country does not fall apart over the next stretch of time. Kindness and love must prevail.

November 19, 2016

The first fall of snow is here.

Costa Rica was wonderful. It was relaxing and joyous to be there for Abby and Rodrigo's wedding. They set up a table with photos of those who could not be present at the wedding because they were no longer with us, and Asher's photo was included. It was touching to see his beautiful face represented when he could not be there himself.

Parts of the trip were hard, though. There was so much joy and celebration. It was hard to not long for Asher to be with us to join in the joy. He will never know on this Earth how much his family loves him.

He will never on this Earth be part of a celebration as wonderful as that wedding.

Snow is falling today, and it brings forth the anticipation of the upcoming holidays, more celebrations that Asher will not be here for. The anticipation is hard and saddening. More than anything, we don't want him to be forgotten. We want (although it's unrealistic) for him to be as mentioned and present as Paisley. But alas, this is wishful thinking that probably won't happen—and understandably so. It's just sad and hard, but inevitable.

I wrote this poem this morning in the hope of bringing to light my feelings:

> With the first fall of snow comes mourning
> With the first fall of snow comes a broken
> heart
> With the first fall of snow comes a reminder
> of those not present
> With the first fall of snow comes
> anticipation of celebrations that will not
> be whole
> With the first fall of snow comes wind that
> blows the chimes of sorrow and memory

With the first fall of snow comes the
    stillness of loss
With the first fall of snow comes longing for
    the baby boy who is not in our arms

November 27, 2016

Our first major holiday without Asher came and went. We thankfully/blessedly/miraculously made it through in a positive and joyful way.

We brought "Asher's Candle" (purchased specifically for this trip to Ohio) thanks to the advice we got from Cori. At large family gatherings, she and her husband bring their daughter's candle and light it to represent Norah since she isn't present physically. They also use this candle at home to wordlessly signify to the family when they are having a day filled with thoughts of Norah.

While we didn't announce the meaning of the candle to all present, our immediate family knew why it was lit, and it brought peace and comfort to know that Asher was being remembered.

Everyone was supportive during a time that could have been very hard for both Betsy and me. Because of that, we occasionally talked freely of Asher in a positive way with no tears. We had a nice time, and that's all we could have hoped for.

December 7, 2016

L ife can be filled with so many ups and downs. One thing that's so hard about losing a child is that all the "downs" seem much greater than they may have been without constant, underlying grief. Another is that the "ups" seem less prominent for the same reason.

Some downs happening now seem petty and minor but when added up can be overwhelming. Currently, we are dealing with Leo and Louie peeing in the house because of the cold weather. They will go outside if we take them out, but they won't use the dog door anymore because they don't want to go out in the chill. Because of this (we are guessing), our cat, Clara, is marking in our house to claim territory. Cleaning up urine seemingly constantly is putting strain on our life.

We can't deal with three animals peeing (especially with how foul cat urine is), so we are considering finding Clara a new home where she can be happy and get the love she deserves.

We also have the underlying financial struggle in our lives. Like most young couples, we are dealing with having little money but still needing to make house payments, pay our bills, and buy food. We've been trying to make any cutbacks we can, but our financial struggle is finally catching up with us in a more acute fashion. The amount of money that we bring in just barely covers our bills (usually). Any other expenses we have get put on the credit card, and our limit is getting dangerously close.

Our long-term plans are for Betsy to go back to school for massage therapy, so she can begin her career as soon as possible. We are currently pursuing this and are on the right track for her to start school in January. However, this doesn't change our financial situation. It's something that we will need to continue to work through.

Betsy and I talk frequently about the concept that I've called "spiraling." If one thing goes wrong, we begin to think of other things that are also wrong, and those thoughts inevitably come back to Asher and his absence from our lives. Days when spiraling happens are very challenging. The grief often overwhelms us and makes life seem unbearable. This is a struggle that we will keep working to overcome, or at least learn the best ways to counteract.

A few days ago, Harper Funeral Home (the funeral home that helped us with Asher's cremains, etc.) held a memorial service for all of those who passed away this last year. It was a lovely service. Betsy and I were there together with my parents, Ashton, Ryne, Paisley, and Brittney. I am so thankful that they attended. The funeral home also gave us a nice ornament inscribed with Asher's name and birth year.

We have also been trying to decide when an appropriate time to start trying to conceive another child will be. The discussion of money, school, and timing has been going on for a while. After a good discussion that we had the other night, Betsy and I decided that it's time. We are trying again! This is exciting but extremely terrifying. We now have to worry about the stress of conceiving and bearing a child when we know full well that we may lose that child at any time. We are trying to avoid thinking about that now.

In other good news (one of this week's "ups"), a book that I contributed to called *From Father to Father* was released! It's a book of letters compiled by Emily Long written by fathers who have lost a child to other fathers in a similar situation. I highly recommend purchasing a copy of the book as it includes letters from many fathers, not just me. More perspectives and stories can help bring more comfort and understanding.

December 8, 2016

I finally finished *Vessels: A Love Story* by Daniel Raeburn today. While it was an interesting, compelling, raw read, it was not what I expected or hoped for.

It's an excellent book that I would recommend to people looking to feel someone else's experience of love and loss. But I did not find it comforting. It was real. It was raw. It was emotional. It was heavy. But not comforting.

I certainly do not regret reading it, but I hope that others who read my writing may find some comfort in my words. I write not only hoping that others will find my words real, raw, and compelling, but also hoping that they will find comfort in knowing that there is someone else in the world who can relate to their loss and grieving.

To all readers of these words: know that there are people in the world (myself included) who care about you. Know that there are people who can empathize with you. And know that in times of hardship, loss, and grief, goodness will once again return to your life if you seek your allies out and hold us close.

January 3, 2017

It's been a while since I've written, and it seems that so much has happened in such a short amount of time.

First of all, one stress in our lives has gone. After having enough of our animals "going" in the house, we found Clara a new home. My cousins' step-sister and her family were a great match for Clara. While it was sad to see her go, I know that they will take good care of her and give her the love and attention she deserves. It's odd, though, to consider the alternative if we hadn't lost Asher: we would not have our dogs and Clara would be the pet who he grew up with. Now our next child will never know her and grow up with Leo and Louie instead. It's not bad by any means—it's just odd to think about.

Finances are a big factor in determining the next step in our lives. I wish it wasn't so, but money is a large driving factor in our lives right now. We need money to live, keep our standard of living, save for future children, and prepare money for future prospects. Money is tight right now, but I think some methods (which I won't bore you with) that we've chosen can lead to a stable future.

The biggest upcoming change is that in a few weeks, Betsy is going back to massage therapy school. Getting back into something she loves is an excellent move for her. She also does well with having a busy schedule. Not to mention (of course) that it will be a big financial help for her to have a career when she finishes school. I'm excited to see what this venture brings her and our family.

We also decided a couple of weeks ago to start trying to get pregnant again. While the official "wait time" to get pregnant again after a C-sections is one year, nine months is pretty close, and most sources say that it is okay to get pregnant again at this time.

Unfortunately, pregnancy (and even potential

pregnancy) comes with its own stresses. Betsy and I have never had a successful pregnancy. Our only child did not make it. We know all too well what could happen with future pregnancies. Losing another child would be unthinkable. I know we would make it through…We've done it before. But the pain of another loss may be too much. The word "devastating" doesn't do the idea justice. When we are blessed to conceive another child, we will be engulfed by a new wave of stress. The Pregnancy After Loss support group will be invaluable, and we will need a lot of support from those around us. There will be no relaxing until our child is born alive and healthy. One day (hopefully soon), we will know what that relaxation feels like.

School ended well before winter break. We were all ready to be done. Students, teachers, administrators, custodians, everyone. Our first days off were relaxing and we began our many Christmas celebrations.

Because we spent Christmas with my family this year, we started off the festivities with my dad's side of the family early in the month. We anticipated immense grief because our child would be the only one missing from the festivities. However, the day was easier than we thought it would be. Of course, we still experienced sadness but much less than we anticipated. The size of the group helped; we could "hide" if needed or only interact with whomever we wished. Neither course of action was needed, though. It was a good day.

Christmas on my mom's side of the family was a little different, but again, not as bad as we anticipated. For both celebrations, we felt Asher's presence a little more deeply. Since Paisley, Ezra (my cousin's son), and Asher are the only great-grandbabies, Asher's absence was much more acute. There were plenty of distractions, but I still frequently found myself gazing into nothingness, thinking about my son and how he wasn't there to experience the family's love in the same way the other babies were. I love Paisley and Ezra, but they were a reminder this year that one of our number was missing. I fear that they will always be reminders. It isn't fair to them. I pray that the grief will ebb in future years.

Christmas morning, though, was hard. Very hard. Nothing was as it "should have been." Betsy and I woke up and didn't know what to do. We didn't have a child to take downstairs to unwrap presents. We weren't able to share Betsy's Christmas Book with our son for the first time. We didn't have time as a complete family before going to my parents' house for brunch. Tears fell freely that morning.

Again, we anticipated this. In my anticipation, I reached out to other members of our support group to see what they did to remember their lost children on Christmas morning. I got some great suggestions (we were already planning on lighting Asher's candle), but in the end, I decided to try something just for Betsy and me instead.

When we woke up, we went down to open our stockings and give the dogs their treats. Since Betsy's family has a tradition of reading on Christmas morning, we then sat down to read Betsy's Christmas Book. We read it by ourselves this year. Betsy cried throughout. Following that, I read this poem:

My First Christmas in Heaven

I see the countless Christmas trees around
    the world below,
With tiny lights, like Heaven's stars, reflecting
    on the snow.
The sight is so spectacular. Please wipe away
    that tear,

For I am spending Christmas with Jesus
    Christ this year.

I hear the many Christmas songs that people
    hold so dear,

But the sounds of music can't compare with
    the Christmas choir up here.

I have no words to tell you, the joy their
    voices bring,

For it is beyond description to hear the
    angels sing.

I know how much you miss me. I see the
    pain inside your heart,

But I am not so far away. We really aren't
    apart.

So be happy for me dear ones. You know I
    hold you dear,

And be glad I'm spending Christmas with
    Jesus Christ this year.

I send you each a special gift from my
    heavenly home above.

I send you each a memory of my undying
    love.

After all, "love" is the gift more precious
    than gold.

It was always most important in the stories
    Jesus told.
Please love and keep each other as my father
    said to do,
For I can't count the blessings or love he has
    for each of you.
So have a Merry Christmas, and wipe away
    that tear,
Remember, I'm spending Christmas with
    Jesus Christ this year.
—Author Unknown

Following the poem, we sat on the couch for a while and held each other. Our grief permeated the crisp morning.

We then packed to spend the day at my parents'. Brunch was great—it was nice spending time with my family, and we spent most of the afternoon and evening playing games. We brought Asher's ashes with us. We wanted him to be there. I could feel his presence throughout the day.

Betsy's birthday is the day after Christmas. She didn't feel like celebrating this year. I think she may have thought that it just "wasn't right" to celebrate without her son. We did our best to just have a pleasant day (which included buying a new board game) and prepare to go to Ohio to see her family the next day. We spent a few relaxing days in Millersburg before heading home for New Year's Eve. It was nice to spend some time with her family before heading back to our "normal life" at home.

Shelby and Isaac had the idea of having a pajama party for New Year's Eve, and we volunteered to host. We had them and some other close friends over. It was a lot of fun, and it was great to ring in the New Year with such good people.

It's now 2017, and I hope and pray that it will be a better year than 2016. While 2016 may be a memorable year for others in a variety of ways, 2016 will always be the year we lost Asher.

On a related note, I want to share some thoughts based on a post that a Facebook friend shared recently about trauma. I feel that it's imperative to remember that it is okay to care for yourself, even if others have it worse.

A therapist said that it's common for people who are abused, neglected, cheated on, etc. to comment on how "others have it worse." In a sense they feel that, since others have it worse, their pain is irrelevant and they are unworthy of care. This is not the case. It is equally true for child loss. Other kinds of child loss are worse, but that does not mean that I don't deserve to be cared for. The same goes for everyone, no matter the circumstances. I frequently remind myself of this.

January 7, 2017

For the last seven months or so, what was to be Asher's room turned into a storage room where we kept a random assortment of things. It had been set up (mostly) as a nursery when we lost him. While we were still in the hospital, both Betsy's family and mine came together to put away all the things in the nursery so we wouldn't have to deal with the pain of it ourselves. Because it was mostly empty, it became the natural place for us to store some things.

It has needed it for a while now, but I finally got around to cleaning it out today. Most of Asher's things are in the closet, but occasionally we took something out—things from the hospital, a memory box, stuffed animals, anything we wanted at the time to remember him by. Those things eventually made it back to the room but not into the closet.

While cleaning, I organized and went through some of those items, including forgotten mementos, programs from Asher's funeral, sympathy cards from friends and family, and mandalas that had been colored for Asher. I read some cards and notes people had written to Asher on the backs of the mandalas they colored for him. The notes to him caused my heart to break and the loss of Asher to wash over me once more, more powerfully than I had felt it for a while.

I have been grieving almost daily and a few tears come on occasion. But reading words written *to* him was different than anything I've experienced for the last stretch of time. Reading words that weren't for Betsy and me. Reading words that were to him and not about him. Reading words of love and broken hearts. Reading words from family and friends who never even got the chance to meet Asher but cared for him deeply. This is what got me.

I sobbed on the floor as I read the notes to my

son. I am thankful that I have those words. It means the world to me to see that others loved him too.

January 19, 2017

I saw this today and wanted to share:

"Grief, I've learned, is really just love. It's all the love you want to give but cannot. All of that unspent love gathers up in the corners of your eyes, the lump in your throat, and in that hollow part of your chest. Grief is just love with no place to go."
—Jamie Anderson

January 27, 2017

Last night, I listened to the full *Hamilton* soundtrack for the first time. Like a lot of people, I've heard a few of the songs before, but I've never sat down and listened to the musical in its entirety. Unlike a lot of musicals, *Hamilton* is through-sung, so there is no dialogue—the plot is pushed along using all music. The whole plot, therefore, is on the soundtrack. While listening, I followed a synopsis of the plot (there are so many fast words that I wanted to make sure I followed the plot properly).

The reason I'm writing this is because of the numerous times that I cried while listening. It's likely that for many people, different parts of the music and plot resonate with them. This resonance can manifest in different reactions: laughter, tears, shock, etc. For me, I've always been a crier—tears during emotional parts, tears after a particularly enjoyable line of music, tears at anything moving to my soul.

I teared up during "Alexander Hamilton," "The Schuyler Sisters," and "Burn" because of the powerful musical moments that resonate with me—purely musical, not plot based. I teared up during "Satisfied" and "The World Was Wide Enough" because the plot resonated with me.

Then there were times that I teared up (or flatout cried) when I had both a musical and plot-based resonance. "That Would Be Enough," "It's Quiet Uptown," and "Who Lives, Who Dies, Who Tells Your Story," moved me as only a grieving parent can be moved.

"Who Lives, Who Dies, Who Tells Your Story" made me happy that I've found Betsy, but also made me mourn the day that one and then both of us will pass. It shows how one life can impact the world. The song calls me to reflect on how I may be remembered when my time comes.

"That Would Be Enough" brought back all the

anticipation of being a parent. Looking forward to Asher's arrival was enough to make Betsy and me happy and content at the time. It broke my heart to reminisce and to know now what I didn't know then—that the outcome would not be what we expected.

And then there's "It's Quiet Uptown." It's hard to listen to this song without crying. In it, Hamilton's son was just killed, and Hamilton and his wife need to continue living without their child. Angelica's words speak to parents who have lost a child in ways that no one else can fully understand.

Betsy and I are living through the unimaginable every day. How can anyone imagine losing a child? That's not the way of things. All children should outlive their parents. How can this happen? How is this fair?

But it happens…and we live and continue living trying to make the best out of what life has become.

I cried during this song because the plot hit so close to home. I have lost my son. I have experienced moments that words don't reach. I have endured suffering too terrible to name. I've held my child as tightly as I could. And there are times when I try to push away the unimaginable reality that he is gone.

February 1, 2017

This morning, Betsy got her confirmation that she was not pregnant.

For the last few days, Betsy and I noticed that her monthly cycle was different than normal—no mood swings, etc. She decided to take a pregnancy test a few days back (before her missed period) to see if there were early signs of pregnancy. It came back negative. A couple days passed, and we went to a pregnancy clinic where they could do a medical-grade test (even though it was early) in the hopes that we would get the confirmation and peace of mind. Again, negative.

Betsy had been experiencing some typical "pre-pregnancy" symptoms—cramping on one side of her body, back pain, minor spotting. We were confident that she was, indeed, pregnant. As of yesterday, she was officially "late" based on her previous cycles. The only bleeding she had was minor spotting, which could have been implantation bleeding. We were hopeful.

But no, it wasn't to be this month. This morning she started her cycle.

Because of the different circumstances of this month compared to others, we are confident that Betsy's body tried to become pregnant but, for whatever reason, didn't. A few months before we got pregnant with Asher, a similar situation arose. Same signs, same spotting followed by a delayed period. That time, too, we think that a fertilized egg tried to implant and failed.

Betsy said this to me when we were discussing it today: "I tried to remember that it's probably God's way of stopping a potentially difficult pregnancy before it even begins. I have to believe whenever we get pregnant again, our baby will grow as it should and be healthy."

I think this is a good way to think about an unfortunate situation. We are both sad, but we are confident that we will conceive a child when the time is right.

February 17, 2017

Each day, time passes.

Each day is hard.

Each day, I wish things were different.

Each day, I am thankful for what you've
given me.

Each day, I miss you more.

Each day, I think of you.

Each day, you grow fainter in my memory.

Each day, my memories of you become
more ingrained.

Each day, I want you to be with me.

Each day, I want to hold you in my arms.

Each day, I want to see your face in front of
me.

Each day, I want to hear your voice.

Each day, I want to watch you grow.

Each day, I cannot have what I want.

Each day brings me sorrow.

Each day brings me happiness.

Each day, I feel like less of a father.

Each day, I feel more like the father of an
angel.

Each day, life goes on.

Each day, my love grows.

Each day brings me closer to you.

Each day, I move closer to acceptance.

March 7, 2017

Asher's birthday gets nearer every day. I don't know how it will be.

Sometimes, I imagine a day full of sorrow—staying at home, leaving the lights off, crying, looking at pictures, remembering the details of that day.

Other times, I imagine a day full of smiles and joy—getting together with close friends and family, having a party, remembering the joy of seeing my son for the first time.

I don't want either of these things, though. While both may be possible, I'm hoping for a day of love and acceptance. A happy medium between the two would be best—grief for losing what could have been, smiling as we spend time with family and friends, looking at pictures of our son with a mixture of sorrow and joy, some tears and some laughter.

Only time will show what the day is meant to be, though.

Talking with other members of our support group has been helpful. Hearing the stories of how they've done birthdays for their babies, hearing of what they have planned for when the birthday arrives. It seems that I've heard of days full of sorrow, days full of joy, and a lot of days with both.

I want both.

On a related note, I'm thinking of completing this journal on April 11. One year seems like a good timeline for documenting what the life of a grieving father is like. I know that my life will continue to be filled with ups and downs. I know that there will be more that I want to share. But, although Asher's story is unending, this journal needs an end.

March 8, 2017

My heart is acutely aware of Asher's absence today. I am a father, but I am not fathering a child. My soul has a compulsion to father a child. And I don't want to wait anymore.

But I have no choice. Waiting is all I can do. I desperately hope that we will get pregnant soon. Very soon.

I have a few colleagues who are currently expecting their own children. Every time I am reminded of their anticipation, I say a little prayer that their child lives. Simultaneously, I push down my jealousy and resentment that others should get to experience parenthood while I do not. I know these feelings are (mostly) irrational. I know that it's not fair for me to be angry that others get to experience happiness when I cannot, but my feelings are what they are. I am happy that they won't go through what Betsy and I have been through, but I am sad that I didn't get their positive experience.

Bringing another child into the world will help allay these feelings. Fathering a child will bring some peace to my soul.

This is my hope.

March 20, 2017

Sometimes reminders come out of nowhere and punch me in the gut. I immediately feel distanced from reality. My vision goes unfocused, there's an ache in my heart, my brain slows down, my thoughts are fuzzy and clear at the same time as I think about Asher. I am never prepared for these moments, but they happen nonetheless.

Yesterday, I was playing trumpet for a church service. During the service, a baby started making noise. Not crying; just baby sounds. And it punched me.

Earlier in the day, I saw a man talking to his

baby boy who was only a few months old. He was just talking to him. And it punched me.

Today during a staff meeting, a pregnant teacher gave a presentation. I've seen her large, pregnant belly before, but halfway through her presentation I thought of Betsy's pregnant belly. And it punched me.

Later during the same meeting, another coworker was talking about making plans to move out of his apartment because his wife is supposed to have her baby soon. A conversation of little consequence. And it punched me.

Later still, two other coworkers were walking down the hallway. One asked the other if he was expecting a baby, to which the first coworker answered, "Yes." One little word. And it punched me.

I wish these punches happened less. But I also don't. The punches are reminders of what has happened, what could have been, what I no longer have, what I will keep with me forever. The punches aren't so debilitating that other people will notice them happen, but they are still acute. I want them to help me remember, but I don't want them because they are painful.

I have a feeling these punches will remain with me forever.

March 24, 2017

I think the time is right for me to start rereading these journal entries that I've been making for the last year. I would like to read Asher's story from my own point of view. While so much of his time with us is in my mind, some of the details have been lost. With his birthday approaching, I want to have the whole experience fresh in my mind. Now, more than ever, I am thankful for the pages I have written.

April 9, 2017

I finished rereading this chronicle of all the events surrounding Asher's short time with us. While I knew what these pages contained, I am still blown away with grief after reliving the memories. I am glad I have his story, so I can revisit it whenever I need to. But reliving it is hard.

Since my last entry, a number of things have happened. I threw Betsy a surprise birthday party, and I had a birthday myself. As expected, the happy occasions were laced with thoughts of Asher and how life would have been if he had been with us. Abby, Kathy, Andy, and Betsy's grandma and grandpa have all visited since then. When I see them, I sometimes suddenly remember that these people have lost their only nephew, grandchild, and great-grandchild. It isn't just Betsy and me who are grieving his loss.

Kristen from support group shared a post on our Facebook page the other day. It's from an author and blogger named Rachel Lewis. I thought it reflected the loss that we and our extended family feel. It's a feeling of loss for everyone but of more than just a baby—it's a loss of an entire life. She writes in a poetic manner about all the things that will not be. She writes of the first time a child rolls over, his first day of kindergarten, her T-ball games, his first crush, wedding dress shopping with her, watching him become a father, and every point of the life that the child no longer has. Rachel really hit the nail on the head. We will forever be grieved by the "not knowing" of what Asher's life could have been. That feeling will never go away.

Right now, Betsy and I desperately want to conceive another child. We need another being in this world who we can give love to in the way we would have given it to Asher. I know that our next pregnancy will be hard—perhaps harder than I imagine—but it will be worth it when we finally have a child with us.

A friend, Jen from our support group, recently had a miscarriage following the loss of her daughter Emerie. She and her husband named their second child Elie. She took a brave step following their second loss and wrote a blog post about their sweet angels and the struggles she was going through. I pray for some comfort for Jen and her husband. Going through another loss is more than I can imagine. No one should ever have to go through this grief again.

I pray that our next pregnancy is a successful one. I don't know how I could handle another loss.

Asher's birthday is in two days. We haven't really planned anything. I've been avoiding the conversation. I expect that it will be organic, and the right thing will come to us. It will be a hard day, but it must come.

The final entry of this journal is drawing near. A year in the life of a childless father is one that I never expected to experience—but I am glad to have it documented.

April 11, 2017

Asher's first birthday.

It's so hard to believe that it has already been a year since I received that life-altering, soul-shattering phone call that my son had died. But here I am. Alive and still moving down the path toward my future.

For more than a month, I've been afraid of what this day would have in store. I've prayed every night for a while now that God would bring Betsy and me peace on this day. God answered my prayers. For many, the first birthday that parents are without their children is filled with grief. I've heard the stories from other members of our support group about the struggles on this day. For me, this day was not a struggle but an occasion to reflect upon our baby's time with us, grieve for the future he doesn't have, and memorialize his memory. Grief was present all day, but it wasn't debilitating. It pushed me forward to ensure that Betsy and I had a day filled with our son's memory.

Emily took the train in last night to be with us. This morning, she, Betsy, and I collectively colored a mandala for Asher. While coloring, the doorbell rang, and I went to go receive the beautiful flowers for Asher that were sent by his Aunt Emily, Uncle James, Aunt Abby, and Uncle Rodrigo. We finished the beautifully colored mandala and went to get it laminated.

We took the mandala to a bit of forest that my parents own and hunted for the right tree. We found its towering form near the edge of the property and hung the mandala from it. Even though we have Asher's ashes with us always, we wanted the opportunity to go somewhere to "visit" him—to make a pilgrimage to a place where we can hold his memory. Each year following this, we intend to color another mandala to hang on the same tree with the others. I look forward to this being a family tradition that we share with our future children.

After our pilgrimage, we went to Fort Wayne to get some lunch. Emily bought a bottle of wine and we toasted Asher's memory. We took some time during lunch to share our memories with him and to express how lucky and thankful we are to have such a loving and kind family.

We went to watch Brittney get her first tattoo afterward. She got a beautiful hand-drawn tree with three birds flying away from its branches. The birds represent Asher and the two babies Ashton lost in miscarriage. It's a beautiful tribute.

Betsy had the idea of planting a tree in Asher's memory. We talked about this in the past, but it never happened. Today was the right day to make it happen. We went to purchase a weeping cherry tree and brought it home. We took the time to dig the hole and ensure that it had all the water it needed. I love that we now have a living entity to carry his memory into the future.

At the end of the day, we sat down to write letters to Asher. I put mine in a sealed envelope, so it was just for him to see. We took our letters and put them inside the memorial box that we have for him in our garden. My parents brought over their letters as well, along with a couple gifts. His Grammy brought him a "Little People" boy (she collects Fisher-Price Little People and thought her grandson should have one of his own). His papa brought him a baseball with his note to Asher written on it. Throughout the day, I hadn't felt the need to cry until I saw the gifts they gave to Asher. I'm so happy that he now has some toys to play with on his first birthday.

The events of today were perfect for the son we've lost.

As this year comes to a close, I look to the future to see what it has in store. I know that even though many things in my life will change, I will never stop grieving for Asher. For the rest of my life, I will always be thankful for the time we had with him, wonder what his life could have been, and look forward to the day when I will see him again.

Before I close this journal, I want to extend a hand of caring, love, and understanding to all grieving fathers. Know that you are not alone in this journey. It may be the most difficult journey you ever embark upon, but you can and will make it through. Find someone to share your child's story with. Share it with anyone and everyone that you need or want to. I am beyond thankful that I journaled throughout this year, so I can share Asher's story with anyone who reads this journal—including myself. If you ever need advice or words of encouragement from another grieving father, contact me by email at kavinjley@gmail.com. I understand, and I will be here for you during this difficult time.

I want to extend the hope of peace and blessings to all who have read Asher's story. Thank you for joining me in remembering my sweet angel.

*The journal is dedicated to
Asher, my son.*

ABOUT THE AUTHOR

Kavin Ley is a devoted husband, friend, music teacher, and father of an angel who left this world too soon. He is an active voice in the child loss community, having recently contributed to the book *From Father to Father: Letters from Loss Dad to Loss Dad*. He continues to share Asher's story in the hope that other parents, particularly fathers, will be encouraged to share the stories of their own children. Kavin currently lives in Auburn, Indiana with his wife Betsy and their two mini-dachshunds, Leo and Louie.

Made in the USA
Lexington, KY
06 April 2018